Grief . . . A Comedy

Alison Larkin

Advance edition published 2024, New York New York USA by Alison Larkin Presents

ISBN 978-1-963452-06-8

Copyright © Alison Larkin 2024

Interior design by Inanna Arthen, inannaarthen.com

Cover design by LNDESIGN

Website www.alisonlarkin.com

Email info@alisonlarkin.com

Instagram @alisonlarkinpresents

www.facebook.com/alisonlarkinfan/

Some names, dates, events and locations have been changed. Apart from that, this story is true.

ABOUT THE AUTHOR

Alison Larkin was born in Washington, D.C., and raised in England and Africa by loving English adoptive parents. When she was in her mid-twenties she found her birth mother in the mountains of Tennessee, moved to New York and became a stand-up comic, because what else do you do?

She is now an internationally acclaimed writer, comedian, podcaster, speaker, and actress. She is the founder of Alison Larkin Presents and the award-winning narrator of over 280 audiobooks, including her hugely popular eighty-one hour recording of *The Complete Novels* by Jane Austen, *Alice in Wonderland* by Lewis Carroll, and the *Agatha Raisin* series by M.C. Beaton. She has won many awards for her audiobook narrations including fifteen AudioFile Earphones Awards for excellence for her narration of *Pride and Prejudice, Sense and Sensibility, Friends for Life, The Secret Garden, Jane Eyre, Peter Pan* and *The English American*. Alison is also host of *The Jane Austen Podcast with Alison Larkin* from Realm.fm and the upcoming podcast, *Love And Laughter After Fifty with Alison Larkin*.

Her bestselling autobiographical novel, *The English American* (Simon and Schuster, 2008), sprang from her hit one-woman show of the same name, about an adopted English woman who finds her birth mother, love—and her self—in the United States.

As a comedian she headlined at The Comic Strip in New York and The Comedy Store in Los Angeles and spent three years under Hollywood studio development contract with CBS, Jim Henson Productions, and ABC to star in her own sitcom.

As an actress she has appeared on and off Broadway. Her unusually wide range of voices can be heard in countless films, games, and cartoons from *Grand Theft Auto 5* to the film *Fargo* to hit cartoons like *The Wonderpets*.

She currently lives, records, and writes from her home in Stockbridge, Massachusetts.

For Bhima, of course

PROLOGUE

I met Archbishop Desmond Tutu in 2005, when I was invited to join him for lunch at a restaurant in New York by Karen Hayes, a mutual friend who was making a documentary about him and staying with me at the time.

The Arch, as his friends called him, was sitting at the head of the table between two Very Impressive Young Men. I was at the far end of the table feeling small and thinking, *What on Earth am I doing here?* Suddenly the Arch stopped the conversation and said to the two Young Men, "I did not win the Nobel Peace Prize to listen to you two trying to impress me by going on and on about yourselves and your accomplishments because you think I might be able to help your careers, while you completely ignore the young woman at the end of the table. Alison, tell us about you."

"Right," I said. "I was adopted by English parents and came to America a few years ago to find my birth mother . . . in Bald Mountain, Tennessee. Then I moved to New York and became a stand-up comic, because what else do you do?"

Everyone at the table laughed.

"Did you have a good adoption?" Archbishop Desmond Tutu asked.

"Yes," I said. "I got lucky. Then again, if I'd been adopted by Mia Farrow, today I could be married to Woody Allen."

The Arch laughed loud and long. Then he invited me to join him and his group over the next two days. We spent the time in between his engagements cracking each other up and when he found out I could do a Margaret Thatcher impression, he insisted I sit opposite him at meals and, with me as "Margaret Thatcher," we had several outrageous political discussions which we both found hilarious.

During a brief break in our repartee, he turned to me with a serious expression on his face and said, "Alison, I am not sure why I am feeling called to tell you this, but I want you to remember something. And it's this: 'I can't control what happens to me. But I can control how I respond to it.'"

Fifteen years later our mutual friend insisted I write an email to Archbishop Desmond Tutu telling him the basics of the story you are about to read.

Here's what happened ten minutes later.

October 15, 2020

Dear Alison,

Of course I remember you. How could I forget the young comic who conversed with me in the voice of Maggie Thatcher with such aplomb?

I also remember what I said to you the following day and am glad that it is helping you now. I loved your comedy and your novel, and I've kept tabs on you over the years.

Alison, your story needs the widest circulation possible because it will bring hope to many people who might otherwise condemn themselves to a life of despair. You must do whatever you have to do to make sure this story is told as widely as possible. And not just in an email to me!

Arch

October 15, 2020

Dear Arch,

Thank you so much for your kind words. I am glad you think my story might be able to help people, but I am sorry to say the thought of writing another book makes me want to hide under the bed and never come out again. I'm with Dorothy Parker, who said, "I hate writing. I love having written."

I know how busy you are. Thank you again for reading my email and especially for taking the time to reply.

Alison

Five minutes later . . .

October 15, 2020

Dear Alison,

So do what you did last time. Write a one-woman comedy show, write songs, tell jokes, whatever. But tell this story! God is smiling and wants to use you powerfully.

Arch

October 15, 2020

Dear Arch,

I am glad you think so, and I'm glad you and God have such a good relationship. I am sorry to say that I don't really believe in God.

Unless God is love and everything that is good, in which case I do believe in God, I just call it by another name.

BTW, I think all religions lead to God. And no religions lead to God.

But I do believe in you and everything you have done throughout your life to help other people. And even though it will be hard to relive the whole story, I will make myself do it. Because you have asked me to.

Alison

October 16, 2020

Dear Alison,

You have put a smile on the face of God, who is very

pleased indeed to hear this. She fully expects you to create something wonderful.

Blessings,
Arch

October 16, 2020

Dear Arch,

So, no pressure then?
Please tell God I will do my best and keep you both posted.

Alison

November 22, 2021

Dear Arch,

I am so very sorry to hear from Karen that you are not well. This is just a quick note to let you know I have just finished writing a new one-person comedy show. It is going to be produced in America in 2022 and in London in 2023. After that I promise I will write a book.

Alison

November 23, 2021

Dear Alison,

May you go from strength to strength putting a smile on the face of God, who is immensely proud of you. You are a star. God bless you, Alison.

Arch

This book is dedicated to the memory of Archbishop Desmond Tutu. So if you don't like it, you can blame him.

CHAPTER 1

People have told me that when someone you deeply love dies, you can sense them with you at first. But after awhile the connection goes away and they don't feel near anymore. Not so in our case, it seems.

Bhimashankar Nitta, my fifty-four-year-old Indian lover, fiancé, kindred spirit, partner, and friend, has been dead for well over a year, but right now he's sitting on the other side of my kitchen table.

Great love stories usually happen to people who meet when they are young. Like Romeo and Juliet. Or my English parents, who met when they were in their early twenties and have loved each other for sixty-four years.

We met in our fifties, for God's sake. And our love story is showing no sign of ending, which is the biggest surprise of all. And there have been a lot of surprises with this, believe you me.

Today, Bhima is wearing his light green lungi and no shirt. The five-inch scar on his chest is still visible, and he's been watching me finish yesterday's Wordle.

"F.O.R.G.E. You got it in two," Bhima says.

"I did!"

It is satisfying, in a world gone mad, to be able to solve something.

Through the kitchen window, behind Bhima's right shoulder, I can see my yellow shed, a.k.a. Audiobook Cottage, from where I have been recording audiobooks since the start of the pandemic. I ought to be narrating Agatha Christie's *The Man in the Brown Suit*, which is due tomorrow, but instead, here I am talking to Bhima again.

When people ask me how I am doing these days, I say, "I'm fine," because I'm English. We English have a bit of a thing with denial. There are, for example, no alcoholics in England. Just people who start drinking a little early—like when they wake up.

I live in a small white house with green shutters, which was built in 1835 in the tiny town of Stockbridge, Massachusetts, the home of Norman Rockwell, Alice's Restaurant, and the Red Lion Inn. It's an achingly beautiful place, populated more heavily since the pandemic drove New Yorkers and folks out of Boston into the heart of New England so they could live less expensively, surrounded by mountains, lakes, and Democrats.

The rich flit away from here to warmer climes when the weather gets cold and come back in May. As for the rest of us— well, when the snow falls at the start of winter I think, *How pretty.* But by the end of February, I'm a freezing depressive with the flu.

It's the end of February 2022. Bhima is trying to get my attention by tapping his long fingers against the side of my kitchen table, which used to be his.

When he died, I told Bhima's family I didn't want anything except the kitchen table and chairs and Bhima's green and cream rug that I disliked while he was alive and now has pride of place in the center of my living room floor.

I don't understand how Bhima is here, or why, but he's been here for at least part of every day since six weeks after he died— and recently he's been showing up more often. Which is not how this is supposed to go.

"Why are you still here?" I ask him, finally.

His brown eyes were so beautiful. Are so beautiful. Were . . .

I can hear the hum of the dishwasher and the hiss of the old metal radiators that clang too loudly whenever the heat goes on. I can hear the clock ticking above the kitchen sink and two boys laughing and throwing snowballs across the road.

"Why are you still here, my love?" I ask again.

And then I hear Bhima's voice as clearly as my own.

"Because, beautiful woman, you're lonely as hell."

What is that old quote I've never managed to wrap my head around? If you don't hear a tree fall in the forest, did it make a sound? Something like that, anyway.

Is this something similar? If you can't see someone, literally, does it mean they are not really there? And what does being "really there" mean, anyway? Aren't we all a mix of thoughts and feelings born from whatever happened, and whatever we imagined happened, to us in our past, mingled with whatever's going on in the present?

Right now, Bhima is as real to me as the guy with the ponytail who cooks fish at the Lenox market. And yet, I want to be with Bhima and don't much like the guy who cooks fish at the Lenox market, who is a bit of a bully.

Now, I'm puzzling over today's Wordle.

"I've tried C.A.C.H.E. but that doesn't work either."

"Try C.A.R.T.E.," Bhima says.

"That's it. Of course!"

Bhima laughs softly. "I'm not sticking around to help you with Wordle, Alison."

"Why are you sticking around?" I say.

He's looking at me fully. "To help you find love again."

CHAPTER 2

"You've been alone for a year and a half. This is not good for you."

As a first-born Indian male, Bhima is used to making pronouncements, and as a first-born English female, I am used to challenging them.

Bhima is lying on my couch with his hands behind his head, waiting for my response.

"I'm not alone," I say. "I see my coffee shop buddies every morning."

Every morning at 7:00 a.m. I head down the hill to Stockbridge Coffee and Tea, buy a dark roast coffee, and chat with the other early risers, all of whom are called Bob. Except for Jessica, who is called Jessica, and who usually arrives a bit later, and Pepino, who is the very Italian chauffeur for the Boston Symphony Orchestra and has been driving the likes of Yo-Yo Ma, John Williams, and Lady Gaga to and from Tanglewood for the past thirty years.

One of the Bobs is an iron monger, another is a doctor, and the Bob I know best used to play drums in the streets and guide tours around Ernest Hemingway's house in Key West. Now, at seventy-eight, he works in a thrift shop in Lee and spends every evening talking to his seventy-eight-year-old girlfriend, an old flame who lives in Maine who he reconnected with last year. He's the happiest older person I know.

Bob drives an old silver VW Cabrio with a leaky roof. But what does that matter? When it rains, you can always wear a hat.

I write and narrate audiobooks all day, which requires solitude, so often my coffee shop buddies are the only people I see.

When the pandemic hit and the coffee shop was offering takeout only, we sat outside wrapped in blankets, wearing several layers beneath our coats and hats.

When the New England weather turned really really cold, Bob "There's No Such Thing as Bas Weather Just Bad Clothing" Wilken brought a fire pit, which helped keep us warm until we were told we had to move it because it was blocking the sidewalk. Which it was.

As a result of our pandemic-induced friendship, I know a great deal about tire pressure, fan belts, alternators, and second-hand cars.

"I'm not alone," I tell Bhima again. "I have my coffee shop buddies. I have the mountains. And I have you."

"You do," Bhima says, "but you are a fifty-five-year-old woman with your whole life ahead of you!"

"Hardly my whole life."

"You're in your prime, baby!"

"So were you."

It's been over a year and we still don't know why he died.

CHAPTER 3

"Alison, I need your help with something," Bhima says. I turn my gaze from the sunlight outside my window toward Bhima, who is lying on my couch again. I can get lost for hours looking at sunlight on snow these days. There's something about the golden light that draws me, especially when the wind lifts the snow into whirling spirals specked with diamonds. But when Bhima demands my attention, he gets it.

"I've been working on a puzzle," he says.

"Oh, yes?"

"Usually I can solve puzzles pretty quickly, but this one has me flummoxed."

I love the way Bhima uses words like "flummoxed." And old-fashioned British phrases, like "Oh my giddy aunt." Once, when I asked him how he wanted his toast, Bhima actually said, "With lashings of strawberry jam."

"Enid Blyton!" I said.

"Yes!"

"Let's celebrate by drinking lashings of ginger beer," Bhima said, as delighted as I was to be in the same room as someone else who understood this obscure childhood reference.

Hearing Bhima say quintessentially British phrases in his thick South Indian accent always makes me laugh.

"Alison," Bhima says again, here, now, today.

"What, my darling?"

The light dances on my laptop.

"The puzzle!"

"Okay, tell me about this puzzle, Bhima," I say.

The light from the lamp is reflected in his eyes. Narnia, our fat black cat, is lying on his legs, purring.

Good God, Bhima is giving me his full attention.

This is new. When he was alive and in conversation with me—or anyone, really—Bhima was usually scrolling through his texts at the same time.

"I have never been able to understand why it took someone like you over fifty years to fall fully in love," Bhima says.

"That's the puzzle?" I say, half smiling.

"It is."

Oh God. Really?

"It was in *The English American*," I say, referring to my autobiographical novel.

"Sure, Alison," Bhima says. "But the love story in *The English American*—"

"What about the love story?"

"Well, you made it up!"

"Of course. No one would have been interested otherwise. Anyway, that's what you do when you are writing a NOVEL! You get to write whatever you wish had happened."

"You were beautiful and charming and so alive! You could have had anyone you wanted. And yet you spent twenty years married to a man you didn't love, who you had nothing whatsoever in common with!" Bhima says.

"Yep."

"Why?"

When you meet and fall in love in the way Bhima and I did, and you're me, you don't want to spend all your time rehashing the past. You want to spend it walking about in nature and hearing about each other's day and making love and talking about ideas and cooking and laughing together and playing rummy and sitting outside holding hands under the stars.

"Why did you marry a man you did not love?" Bhima asks again.

"I did tell you some of this," I mutter.

"Not much. And besides, I wasn't always paying attention when I was alive."

"I know." Now it's my turn to laugh.

"But now I've got all the time in the world," Bhima says,

grinning, his head resting in his hands.

My heart flips. If I tell Bhima the whole story, I'll have to relive it all.

In the past, when Bhima would ask me about myself, I'd change the subject or ask about him.

I can't refuse Bhima now, though. Not with that expression on his face, which lights up like a child's when he is really interested in something. He's pacing up and down now, full of life and energy and . . .

"First, tell the story of why it took you so long to find true love, i.e. me," he says. "Then tell the story of US. And then—"

"Then?"

"Then tell what happened afterwards," Bhima says, his eyes alight.

"No one will believe it."

"Who cares, baby?"

"It's alright for you, you're dead," I say crossly. "I've got to carry on living, and there are these rules one must abide by if one wants to be considered sane."

"Come on, Alison! Tell the story. All of it." Bhima is still grinning. "Let's really knock their socks off."

It's 10:30 a.m. I haven't done any recording today and there are bills that need paying. But Bhima is still lying on my couch with his hands behind his head, giving me his undivided attention, waiting for me to start.

"Would you like something to drink?" I say. "Oh, right. You're not really there."

That's one perk to the situation, I suppose. At least I won't have to cook or do the washing up.

"Alison! Please! The story!"

"Okay . . ."

I open my laptop and start to type.

"I have never been conventionally beautiful," I begin.

"That's not true," Bhima says, suddenly, looking over my shoulder at the screen.

"If you want me to keep going you can't interrupt."

"You were an absolute knockout when you were younger! I've seen the photos! And you are even more beautiful now."

"Bhima!"

"Well it's true! You might not be conventionally beautiful."

"That's exactly what I said! I said I'm not conventionally beautiful."

"You're not conventionally anything."

"Neither were you! Look, here's the deal. We make the deal now, okay?"

"Alright."

"You let me tell the story as I see it, without interruption, or I won't tell it at all."

"Okay," he says, holding his hands up and laughing. "Okay, baby."

CHAPTER 4

W hy did it take someone like myself more than five decades to find true love, like normal people?

I'm not normal. I never have been.

It started at birth. I was born in the US and adopted by the tidiest people in England, who were living in America at the time.

I, like Thomas' English muffins, was packaged as English, but made in the USA.

My English parents had been married for six years when they were told they couldn't have children. They were living in Washington, D.C., where Dad had just been offered a job with the World Bank, but when they found out they had to establish residency in the UK in order to adopt a child there, Dad withdrew his application.

Not wanting to lose the charming, good-looking man with the British accent and his classy English wife, who looked like a brunette Doris Day, Dad's wannabe American boss said, "We do have babies in America, you know."

And that's how it happened.

※ ※ ※

"There's a baby girl who's just been born," the woman from the Adoption Foundation told Mum on the phone on April 28, 1963.

"How lovely!" Mum said.

"Unfortunately, something happened at birth that has caused her throat to close up, so she won't eat. She might not make it, Mrs. White."

"Oh dear," Mum said. "Did someone drop her or something?"

"We can't tell you what happened, for confidential reasons, I'm sure you understand. But if she lives, you can take her home."

It was touch and go apparently, so I was kept in a crib in a foster home in Maryland for the first two months of my life and, because the foster mother was busy, I was only picked up when they tried, unsuccessfully, to get me to eat. During that time, Mum and Dad were allowed to see me twice. Mum wasn't sure how to hold me, and later said she felt rather awkward, but once I began to eat a little, she quite liked feeding me by bottle.

When it was established that the risk of me dying had passed, Mum and Dad took me home.

I look over at Bhima, expecting him to be pleased that I have at least started. Instead he seems tense. I close my laptop and give him my full attention.

Today he's wearing a gold Indian silk outfit embroidered with red that I haven't seen before.

"You were kept in a cage for the first two months of your life?" Bhima says, finally.

"It wasn't a cage. It was a crib."

"Same thing."

"No, Bhima, it really isn't."

"Damn, Alison, you never told me about this," Bhima says.

"It never came up."

"Ripping a baby away from her mother and sending her off to complete strangers with no way of knowing who she came from? That would never happen in India. You'd be given to a family member and raised within the family. We don't put babies in—what did you call it?"

"A crib."

"We don't put babies in a crib in India. I slept with my mother until I was four."

"It was a very reputable adoption agency founded by an attorney," I say.

"Was it?"

"Yes."

"So the 'agency' brokered a deal between the birth parents and the adoptive parents, then strutted off to the bank?"

"No one strutted! I wasn't sold!"

"Did money exchange hands?"

"Some."

"I rest my case."

I close my eyes and picture Bhima asleep with his brothers and sister and parents, all in the same room, cozy, safe, together, connected to their kin.

"If you'd been born in India, you would have been raised by a family member," Bhima says again. "Western culture around this whole issue is barbaric."

"It's different these days."

"And your adoptive parents were British, so let me hazard a wild guess. They followed the 'let them cry it out or you'll spoil them' approach?"

I can almost see my bedroom at the end of the long corridor on the other side of the house from my parents. I can almost see Pooh Bear lying next to me.

"At least I knew I was loved," I say.

"Were you?"

"It depends on what you mean by 'love,' I suppose."

"Did you ever find out the 'confidential' reason why you nearly died?" Bhima says.

"Yes."

He's looking at me in the way he always looks at me when I am not being as forthcoming as he would like. Patient, but with an undertone of exasperation.

"Will the answer help me solve my puzzle?" Bhima says.

"It might."

Bhima allows the silence between us. Then . . .

"So are you going to tell me?"

"I didn't find out myself until I was twenty-eight, and we haven't got to that part of the story yet. So you're going to have to wait."

CHAPTER 5

As is true of all parents, Mum and Dad were my role models in the love department.

The last time I saw him, my eighty-nine-year-old Dad looked over at Mum, to whom he'd been married since he was twenty-three, and said, "Isn't she beautiful? Aren't I lucky?"

For my English parents, true love includes unquestioning fidelity, a sense of humor, and an easy compatibility due to having things in common, like a love of bridge, Scottish dancing, making marmalade, the Lake District, and absolute faith in the BBC.

But despite having this as my role model, as a young woman, whenever I dated a guy I'd find myself on red alert waiting for the object of my affection to leave me, usually by going off with the waitress if I so much as went to the loo. Which I knew was illogical because no one ever did leave me. I left them before they could even think about it.

For me, infatuation was hell.

I did talk to someone about it—but only once.

I was twenty-six and going out with Miles. I urgently needed advice, so I decided to try my father, because a) I trusted him, and b) I reckoned he'd likely know the answer to my quandary because he was, after all, a man himself.

I drove my beaten-up old Renault 5 at top speed from my flat in London to my parents' old country house at the foot of the South Downs in Sussex, three miles from the Cathedral City of Chichester.

I knew Dad must be in the sitting room because I could hear Mozart's Horn Concertos blaring at top volume.

"Hallo?" I called out.

I walked through the kitchen, past the painting of Granny

P. when she was a child, over the maroon Oriental rug that had traveled with our family from England to Washington, D.C., to East and West Africa, to America, then back to England again.

I remember my adrenaline running wildly. I'd never talked to Dad about anything like this, and I knew I'd lose my courage if I didn't do it now.

Dad hadn't heard me arrive and was concentrating intently on putting his CD collection in alphabetical order. I watched him from the doorway, marveling at his ability to take on detail-oriented tasks like this with even a degree of interest.

"Hi Dad."

"Hang on—with you in a minute."

It was now or never.

"Dad, can I ask you something?"

Startled, Dad looked up.

"It's about Miles."

"Ah," Dad said. He turned down the music, stood up, and bellowed for his wife.

"Jilly!"

No reply from Mum.

"Jilly!" Silence. "Mum must be out. Right," Dad said.

"The thing is," I continued, "I think I love Miles. And I think he loves me. But . . . well . . . it's hell, because I'm so afraid he's going to go off with someone else."

I took Dad's deer-in-headlights expression as a sign of encouragement to go on.

"This not being able to trust thing happens every time with boyfriends. And I know it's illogical, because no one ever does go off with anyone else. But I'm so afraid they will, that I pretend I don't like them at all, and then they get confused. And it all becomes a great big mess."

"Ah."

"It's been going on for years."

"I see."

"It's always been like this."

"What?"

"Love. For me. It's always been a kind of hell."

Dad put the CD of the Mozart Horn Concertos back in

its box.

"I'd like to tell Miles the truth about how I'm feeling, but I don't want to put him off."

"Ah," Dad said again.

Dad was about fifty-five at the time, newly retired from living abroad. He tucked his checked white shirt into his trousers and stood up.

"What do you think I should do?" I said.

Outside the French glass window a robin sat on Dad's birdbath, next to the roses. Dad looked at it for a moment, thinking. Then he turned back toward me.

"Tell no one," Dad said suddenly. "That's my advice! Tell no one."

"Not even Miles?"

"Especially not Miles! Good Lord! He's the last person you should tell! Tell NO ONE," he said again, darkly. "What you're feeling is ridiculous! And admitting to something like this will put you in a much weaker position. I say, keep it to yourself and pull yourself together."

Then he smiled kindly, patted me on the back, and left the room.

CHAPTER 6

B hima is laughing. "I love your father!"

"I know."

"His advice was quite Indian, actually."

"You think?"

"Sure. Stoic, stiff upper lip, and all that."

"Yes."

"And unless Miles was a really great guy—like *moi*," Bhima says raising his eyebrows and smiling.

"Like *toi*." We're both grinning now.

"Like *moi*," Bhima says again. "Unless Miles was a really great guy, it was probably good advice."

"You think?"

"I do."

"Americans would not agree with you."

"No, they would not." He chuckles.

"I never told my parents how I was feeling about anything after that."

"Which turned out to be a good thing," Bhima says. "If you'd been able to talk to them, you would have been able to talk about your reunion with your birth mother, and you wouldn't have had to write *The English American*. So . . ."

He has a point.

"I've often wondered what would have happened if I'd married Miles," I say.

"What was he like?"

"Posh, went to Eton College at the same time as Boris Johnson. Self-centered, not very good at communicating, but, like his father, eccentric, difficult, attractive, and interesting. A few years after I left England, I heard he'd set up his own company and become a multi-millionaire."

"Did you love him?"

"I thought I did."

"Then why did you end things?"

"I didn't trust him."

"Why not?"

"He said he wasn't sure, if he got married, that he could promise he would stop going to prostitutes."

"Whaaaaaaaaat?"

"That's what I thought. So I ignored his pleas to talk about the situation and I cut off contact. I've often wondered if I made a mistake. If it was just my insecurity speaking."

"No. You were right to get out."

"Yes, I suppose I was."

"If you'd married this Miles character, you'd have been miserable. And you never would have gone to America to find your birth parents."

"If you'd married one of the young Indian women your parents were trying to arrange a marriage with, you never would have gone to America to get your PhD. And you never would have met me."

"And," Bhima says, "you never would have met me."

CHAPTER 7

I began to wonder if my inability to fully trust the men I was dating might have something to do with my having been adopted. And maybe, just maybe, if I were to find out that it wasn't so much that my birth mother didn't want to keep me but that she simply COULD not—well, maybe that would somehow free me up to live and love like normal people.

So, at the age of twenty-eight, while my friends were getting married to men who looked like David Beckham, I went on a quest to find my birth mother, about whom I knew nothing at all.

I realize that some people reading this will want to know how I found her and what happened, etc. But that would take a book to explain. Oh, wait! I've written one.

So if you want to know more about what that was like, you can read *The English American*, my autobiographical novel about finding my birth parents and my "self" in the USA.

For now, it is enough to say that I learned I was the product of a great love affair between a married man and an unmarried woman who met in the lobby of the Waldorf Hotel at the age of twenty-three, and fell madly in love at first sight.

They were both young Republicans who supported the Christian Coalition. In fact, I was the product of one of their Christian Coalitions.

❈   ❈   ❈

So what IS true love?

Is it born from having things in common? Or is born from an all-consuming passion you are powerless to resist?

And is it just human nature to long for what you don't have?

So, if you're in a loving relationship that's a bit . . . well . . . dull, then maybe you're longing for passion?

Or, if you're in a passionate relationship with lots of angst and drama, maybe you're tired of having your heart yanked around by someone who doesn't know what they want and rather wish you could be in a relationship with someone you can trust?

Did meeting my birth mother instantly solve my problems in the love department?

In a word: No.

❋ ❋ ❋

I'm on Virgin Atlantic Flight 001 to America, flying from the life I know to meet the woman who gave birth to me. And I know that in eight hours' time, my life will never be the same again. And I know what meeting my birth mother will be like, because I have seen it in the movies. We will walk toward each other in slow motion and our souls and hearts will join.

The life I've lived thus far, feeling separate and different, will be over in an instant. I will, at last, feel connected to my own kind.

Our moment of meeting will mark the end of insecurity and mistrust and the birth of an angst-free life.

As I push my luggage through airport arrivals, I watch my body from above, eagerly anticipating my perfect future.

And then, all of a sudden, there she is. The long lost mother I've fantasized about all my life.

She's tall, pretty, looks about thirty-five, has a Southern accent, and she's wearing overalls, like me. Now she's coming toward me at top speed. Now she's holding me in her arms while I'm still carrying two bags.

Now she steps back and says, "Did they tell you you had a twin?"

"Uh . . . no," I say.

"Well you did. You had a twin! Only, he died in the womb. Elvis Presley had a twin who died in the womb, and so did Liberace, so you're in good company. Now where did I park the car?"

Later, I met an adoption psychologist who looked at me with pity, shook her head and said, "Early childhood abandonment

AND twin loss? You're doomed."

From that moment on I knew that love was something other people would do. Like cleaning a kitchen.

And so from this point, if I met someone I was attracted to, who made me laugh deeply or felt like a kindred spirit of any kind, I'd avoid them. Either by throwing myself into my work to the point of exhaustion, or by heading into the arms of someone safe but dull and re-reading *The Road Less Traveled* by Scott Peck. This book, according to my interpretation, is an effective manual on how to talk yourself into tolerating a relationship with someone you don't connect with at all because he's the sort of chap who, on paper, looks like he might be good for you.

CHAPTER 8

"So you had no idea you had a twin until you met your birth mother?" Bhima says

"No. But . . ."

There were things I did not mention to Bhima when he was alive because he was a scientist. But now—hey, he must at least be open to hearing about this stuff now or he wouldn't be sitting at my kitchen table badgering me for clues to his damn puzzle.

"When I was nineteen, I wrote a two-person play," I began. "I had forgotten about this play—it was unfinished—and I'd written it in a notebook that I shoved into a box that lived under my bed for a few years. I found it again soon after I met my birth mother."

"What was the play about?"

I'm a bit nervous about telling him.

"I put it in my novel, *The English American*, but that was technically fiction so no one knew that part was actually true."

"Remind me, Alison. I read it a long time ago."

"Okay. In the play, there were these two characters in a womb. And they were knocking on the walls of the womb saying, 'The walls are shaking. I wonder what's going on out there today?' It was a comedy. I called it *Womb Mates*."

"Of course you did."

"And . . ."

"And?"

"And at the end of the play one of the twins died. So I think an unconscious part of me did know I had lost a twin . . . When you were alive, you would have said it was just a coincidence," I say, finally.

"Not anymore, Alison."

"There were other things, too."

"Like?"

"Okay. During the first two weeks of August 1983, I'm at the Edinburgh Festival with an acting group from university. The director cast me as Louisa in a musical version of *The Duenna*, opposite Mark Strong.

"THE Mark Strong? The good-looking actor in all those movies?"

"Yes."

"Did you kiss him on stage?"

"I did. But it was all acting. You know I've never been attracted to very good-looking men," I say to him.

"Thanks."

"Mark's a great guy, but you're much more attractive, Bhima."

"Too late. But you may proceed," he says, grinning.

"So we're staying in a boarding school outside the city center in dormitories. And Tom Ferborne, who I had recently broken up with, is sleeping with his elegant new girlfriend, Sally Smaller, in the room next door. They always had their arms around each other and, because we were living and eating in the same place and had the same friend group, there was no escape.

"No one knew how I was feeling, because I cracked a lot of jokes, but my heart was breaking. The only time I allowed myself to cry was at night when no one could see. I'd started dreaming about my birth mother again, who either sat by my bed, or floated above it in a long white dress with an expression of pure understanding on her face.

"Anyway, in addition to living together, we also had to see each other in rehearsals for a play called *The Humble Bumble*, in which I was playing Jemima, a bee who spilled everything and knocked things over wherever she went."

"Wild guess. The part was written for you?" Bhima says.

"Indeed it was. Anyway, one afternoon the doorbell to the old school we were staying in rings over and over again. I'm not needed for rehearsal that day so there's no one else around. It's raining, so I run down the old oak staircase and answer the door.

"There's a woman on the doorstep. She's tall and thin and she seems anxious.

'Can I help you?' I say.

'I used to go to school here. I wanted to take a look at the old place again.'

She has an American accent and she's drenched. I take her umbrella, put it in the big pot next to the door, and gesture for her to come in.

Why would an American go to school in Scotland?

Suddenly I'm on alert.

She looks quickly around the room, then back at me.

'I'd be happy to show you around,' I say. And I lead her up the staircase to the rooms above.

She follows me into the main dormitory, looks at the cast-iron beds in various states of disarray, moves past the cedarwood cabinet, and looks out the tall windows over the famous Scottish city.

Then, after a long glance at me, she says, 'I came to lay a few ghosts.'

Could it be HER? The birth mother I know nothing about except that she's American and tall? Has she found me?

I follow her down the stairs, and as she's getting her umbrella from the pot beside the door, I look her intensely in the eyes and say, 'Are you sure you don't need anything else?'

She holds my gaze for a moment.

Then, as quickly as she arrived, she thanks me again and she's gone.

I run to the door and out into the rain. I stand at the end of the narrow street she just turned down. I see her white car stop at the end of the street for a long moment as she looks back in the direction of the school and then drives on.

Fortunately, something stopped me from rushing forward and saying to this complete stranger, 'Mother, Mother! You've found me!'

It wasn't her, of course. But nine years later, when I met my birth mother, she told me she had spent the first two weeks of August 1983 seeing plays at the Edinburgh Festival. And she clearly remembered laughing at a play about a very clumsy bee."

❋ ❋ ❋

Bhima has moved over to the white rocking chair and is sitting with his legs crossed and his arms folded in front of his chest. In this moment he could be mistaken for a Hindu god sitting on top of a pile of clean laundry.

"I wonder," Bhima says suddenly.

"What?"

"If sensing things like this is something you've always done. I wonder if that's why you can be with me now? I have friends who tell me they can't reach the people they love."

"You have friends?"

"Sure. But they don't all get to connect with their beloved in the way we can."

"Why not, do you think?"

"Because their loved ones don't believe in this stuff."

"In the way you used to NOT believe in alternative medicine?"

Bhima laughs.

"Sure."

"You dismissed centuries of Chinese medicine, insisting the whole thing was a placebo! I told you those brown Chinese pellets saved my life!"

"And I told you they saved your life because you thought they could save your life."

"Which is dismissing Chinese medicine!"

"No it's not. If you believe it works, then often it works. The mind-body connection and all that."

"'If you think you can or you think you can't, you're right,'" I say. "Henry Ford. He was adopted."

"Perhaps being adopted is another reason why you can be with me now."

"What do you mean?"

"Well, think about it. You were separated from the birth parents you knew nothing about just after you were born. And yet a part of you always felt connected to them. You were connected to them. I mean, you were carrying around their DNA."

"Go on," I say.

"Your blood relatives were in the world, but you could not see them. You were in the world, but they could not see you."

"But when we met, we recognized each other."

"So maybe what happened to you when you were a baby helped you develop the ability to connect with people later on who are not there physically. Like after they die, for example."

A moment of silence. "Maybe."

CHAPTER 9

After I met my birth mother and then my birth father, I moved to New York and became a stand-up comic. Because what else do you do?

The best thing about stand-up is that you can talk about anything you want as long as you can figure out a way to make it funny. I didn't know anyone in New York, so I started telling comedy club audiences about the surreal thing that had just happened to me.

"Hallo," I'd begin in my very English accent. "My name is Alison Larkin, and I come from Bald Mountain, Tennessee. I arrived in America six weeks ago to meet the mother who gave birth to me for the very first time. You see, I was adopted and brought up in England, and before I met her I thought I was English. But I'm not. I'm a redneck."

This wasn't strictly true; she wasn't a redneck. She was actually from a well-to-do Southern family and a proud descendent of Governor Spotswood of Virginia, but saying I was a redneck in my English accent was funnier.

Someone once said that the proof that there is a God is the fact that I'm still alive, despite some of the things that have happened to me in a car and on the streets. I talked about these real-life incidents in my act.

"I hate driving on the right-hand side of the road. So I don't do it. Much to the annoyance of those very aggressive men in yellow taxis. They keep leaning out of their windows and shouting at me and saying, 'Read the fucking sign, motherfucker!'

"So I'm driving around New York going, 'Read the fucking sign motherfucker, read the fucking sign motherfucker. There IS no fucking sign, motherfucker.' I like saying 'motherfucker.' It makes me feel frightfully New York."

Stand-up was all-absorbing and took my mind off my increasingly troubling relationship with my birth mother.

Soon I started landing roles in cartoons, on Broadway, and in commercials, making more money in an afternoon than I'd made as an actress in England in a year. I was getting booked at Carolines and The Comic Strip and the Boston Comedy Club down on West 3rd Street. I was never bored, and I was rushing around New York so much, I didn't have time to think.

It was the mid 1990's and New York was crackling with danger. But I never felt unsafe in the clubs. Not for a minute.

I was often the only woman on the same lineup as people like Marc Maron and Dave Chappelle.

Dave taught me how to play basketball in our manager Barry Katz's office with crumpled up newspaper. Barry was a former doorman turned comedy manager who, whenever he saw me, pointed an imaginary clicker in my direction and had me flip from accent to accent.

I remember sitting with Dave on the steps of the Boston Comedy Club one night after I watched him roll a joint on stage and share it with the people in the front row.

It was about midnight. A car drove past the club and aimed a red dot at my forehead. Dave pushed me suddenly out of the way. The men in the car drove off laughing.

"You're English, right? Like the Beatles," Chris Rock said one night.

"Not exactly."

If I'd tried to develop as a comic with an accent like mine in England at that time, they'd have told me to fuck off back to my Cordon Bleu cookery, which is ridiculous considering the fact that I really can't cook. But in New York, all that mattered was whether or not you got laughs. And I did.

Sometimes the other comics asked for my input.

"Hey, Alison, why am I not getting a laugh on this?"

"It'll be funnier if you move 'suck my dick' to the *end* of the sentence."

CHAPTER 10

My relationship with my birth mother was exhausting and overwhelming. I was smoking two packs of cigarettes a day and I wasn't eating much.

That was when I met a kind, quiet, older man called Brian who took care of me and didn't fill my head with confusing things. I knew he wouldn't go off with a younger woman because *I* was a younger woman. Plus, he knew how to cook roast chicken and keep order while I ran around to comedy clubs in New York City, and later LA.

So I married him.

My stand-up act evolved into a one-woman show, which led to three years in Hollywood under studio development to star in my own sitcom—once with Jim Henson Productions and ABC TV, and then with CBS Studios.

It was heady, exciting stuff. I got to meet the Muppets. I was being paid not to act on television while the networks developed my show. Mitzi Shore, who owned The Comedy Store on Sunset Boulevard, made me a paid regular.

"The Comedy Store was where Jim Carrey and Robin Williams started, wasn't it?" Bhima says.

"It was."

Being "passed" by Mitzi meant you got stage time, which was what you needed to get good.

I got to see the greats close-up. Frequently, Rodney Dangerfield pretended to just "happen" to be in the crowd. The emcee would spot him there and ask him to come up on stage. He'd say "no no," the emcee would plead, the crowd would go wild, then he'd "reluctantly" head on to the stage to try out twenty minutes of new material.

I was a long way from England.

"So tell them the story about you and Andrew Dice Clay," Bhima says.

"Oh yeah," I say. Bhima is laughing quietly in the corner.

It was my first night at The Comedy Store on Sunset Boulevard, about ten o'clock on a Monday and there weren't many people left in the Original Room—maybe twenty or so. Andrew Dice Clay was on stage trying out his dirtiest material ever. Funny as hell but unquotable and so offensive half the room had just left.

There was no way I could follow that with material. So I walked up to the mic and said "Our Father, who art in Heaven, Hallowed be thy name," and then I walked off.

Mitzi laughed when she heard about it and gave me more and more stage time.

"Were you happy?" Bhima says.

I think back, remembering the smell of stale alcohol, the jagged air in the room where some of the comics did cocaine, the black walls in the corridor with the names of all the comedians who had passed through there.

I remember the crowds that were usually drunk and who, for whatever reason, actually gave me their phones when I asked for them. I'd call the last number dialed, put the person on speaker and riff with whoever was at the end of it.

"Were you happy?" Bhima says again.

"I loved the audiences."

"So why did you give up performing?" Bhima says.

"I didn't. I perform all the time! I've recorded over three-hundred audiobooks Bhima! In which I get to play allllll the parts."

"Yes, but you record them on your own in a soundproof room that resembles a padded coffin. I've seen you go for more than a week without talking to anybody."

"I see my coffee shop buddies every morning and I go to the supermarket."

"When was the last time you hung out with someone under the age of seventy-five?" Bhima says.

"I hang out with you."

Bhima looks at me for a long moment. We breathe.

Then, opening his hands and smiling, he says "Forever

fifty-four."

At first I liked Los Angeles. It's such an optimistic place. Where else would someone pay five million dollars for a glass house on a cliff two weeks after an earthquake?

But then our two children were born.

"Wait a second, you can't just jump to that." Bhima says.

"Why not?"

"What about the pregnancy and all that? Did it just happen at random?"

"Not really."

"As I thought."

Bhima has changed so much since he was alive. He used to pretend to listen, but not quite manage it while he checked his phone, fed the cat, wiped the kitchen surfaces, chopped an onion, or went over his to-do lists.

Here, today, he's still, and he's holding his hands together at his fingertips, giving me his full attention. Waiting.

❈ ❈ ❈

For me, having children was something other people did. Like ironing, I had never even considered it. Then one day I got a pain in my tummy and was whizzed to the hospital. The LA doctor told me that if the problem turned out to be an infection, it could affect my ability to become pregnant. Actually, the problem turned out to be indigestion. But the visit woke me up.

My non-adopted friends had seen their mothers pregnant and knew all about morning sickness and the agonies of delivery. But in my family, babies came ready-made from social workers. You drove to a foster home, a nice lady gave Mum and Dad a new baby, then you all drove home. So up until this point, whenever I pictured the moment when I entered the world, the setting was a wood-paneled station wagon.

I was thirty-five, and I suddenly realized I wanted to have children more than anything else in the world.

But month after month went by and I still wasn't pregnant. Which was a surprise at first. I mean, I thought it would be easy because I wasn't exactly planned. My birth parents were doing everything possible not to get pregnant, and yet I showed up anyway.

My English mother had never been pregnant, and I knew nothing about what happens to a woman's body between conception and birth, so I turned to books for answers. One book said that women who were too thin found it hard to conceive. So I happily gained fifteen pounds. Another insisted that after making love you should lie on the couch for an hour with your legs in the air to make sure no sperm dropped out. It didn't work.

And then, after two years of trying, I was pregnant. Our son was conceived one joyful night after a packed-out performance of my one-woman comedy at the Manchester Royal Exchange in England.

I was in awe of the fact that there was a human being growing inside me. How lucky I felt. And how guilty.

"Why guilty?" Bhima says.

"Unlike the mother who raised me, I got to grow my own baby. Unlike the mother who gave birth to me, I got to keep it."

"Okay, I get it. Proceed."

For me, pregnancy was a glorious time. I went to a pregnancy yoga class so I could be around other pregnant women for the first time, who I watched with fascination.

I approached women with children everywhere—at The Coffee Bean, in Trader Joe's, at the North Beach playground in Santa Monica—and asked them how their deliveries had gone. And, probably because I was pregnant and had an English accent, they would tell me everything, filling in the gaps in my knowledge that Mum could not.

Of course, there was the occasional blip, like the time the yoga teacher asked us to visualize our own birth. At first I pictured a wood-paneled station wagon, but then I went somewhere else.

"Where?"

My heart is beating extra fast as I remember. The yoga room in West Hollywood has been darkened. There are candles. There are other pregnant women lying down peacefully around me. The teacher asks us to be still and breathe and go back and remember the time of our own birth, moments before we came into the

world. Suddenly, from a deeply meditative state, I scream, scare
the hell out of everyone including myself, apologize profusely, get
up and leave.

"What happened, Alison?"

Bhima has come over to the couch and is sitting right next
to me. I can feel his leg just touching mine and the smell of something. Orange? Persimmon? Something like that.

Outside it's been raining, so I can see swirls of mist coming
off the mountain. When the kids were young, whenever we saw
the mist on the way to school I'd say, "Look! The wizards have
been up all night stirring their cauldrons so they can spread good
magic over the Berkshire Hills."

"What did you see when you imagined your own birth,
Alison?" Bhima says again.

I've not told anyone before, but Bhima isn't going to let me
skate over this, so I might as well get it over and done with.

I did as I was told and, guided by the teacher, I lay in the
yoga room picturing the womb.

I'm sharing the womb with my twin brother.

I don't want to leave him behind, but I'm being forced
toward the outside world.

I keep reaching back so he can come with me, but he's not
moving and I'm being pulled, pulled, pulled away.

Then I have no choice. Forces far stronger than I am are
pushing me out, out, out toward a glaring fluorescent light into a
world that I must live in without him.

"Thank you, Alison," Bhima says after a long moment. "Part
of the puzzle is now solved."

"Is it?"

"Yes. Now I know that from the moment of your birth, you
learned that love and connection would result in loss. That ex-
plains a lot."

"I suppose it does."

"The next part of the story will tell us who saved you from
mistrusting love for the rest of your life. And then . . ."

"Then?"

"Then we'll get to my favorite part of the story. Where you
meet me."

CHAPTER 11

Just after my son, Tom, was born in the Good Samaritan Hospital in downtown LA, I saw the shadow of a woman reaching toward him to take him out of the room.

"Excuse me," I said. "Who are you and what are you doing?"

"I'm taking the baby away to be washed," the nurse said.

"No," I said. "You're not. He stays here with me."

"That wasn't very Alison of you!" Bhima says.

"No, it wasn't," I say. "But I was damned if some strange woman was going to take my baby out of my sight for an instant."

And then, despite the fact that they wanted to keep me for four days after my twenty-hour labor and emergency cesarean, I insisted on going home.

For my children there would be no bright lights, no sterilized hands ripping mother and newborn apart, no social workers. They would have a connected, loving, and completely safe beginning to their lives. For the first few weeks with both children I stopped picking up the phone and retreated from the outside world, so it could be just us, bonding in peace.

I close my eyes and remember that golden time, sitting in the rocking chair singing to my children while nursing first Tom and then Lucy in the quiet of the tiny flat we were renting on the edge of Santa Monica.

I spent the early days of Tom's life outside, carrying him in a sling or on my back, walking down to the beach, sleeping on the grass with Tom next to me, always making sure he felt close and loved and wanted.

When Lucy was born, I carried her on my back so she could see the world but stay close and connected to her mother for as long as she needed.

"So instead of putting them in a crib at the end of a corridor, you slept in the same room as your children?"

"Yes."

"And when they cried?"

"I picked them up and held them until they stopped."

"Very Indian!" Bhima says, delighted.

"Yes."

"Do you think you understood them on an instinctive level in a way your adoptive parents were unable to understand you?"

"Yes."

"And because of them, you learned what unconditional love felt like. So that's why, when you met me . . ."

"When I met you?"

"When you met me, you were finally ready."

✳ ✳ ✳

After my children were born, my sense of alarm regarding Los Angeles increased.

My fellow Comedy Store comedian Argus Hamilton summed up my feelings best when he said, "The LA philosophy? 'I may not be much, but I'm all I ever think about.'"

I remember pushing my six-month-old daughter past posters of women with enormous plastic breasts wearing thongs and suddenly knowing, *I can't raise my children here!*

I was under development to star in my own TV show at the time. But I knew I didn't want my kids to grow up in a celebrity culture that values money, youth, and beauty over things that matter.

Plus, I was aware that being famous would mean I'd be under constant pressure to have to brush my hair.

"And that would have meant having to find your hairbrush," Bhima says.

"Correct."

So we made a mistake and moved to New Jersey.

CHAPTER 12

My husband, Brian, was working as a paralegal and I was writing before the kids woke up, then spending the day with them, outside whenever possible.

When Brian came home, he'd head down to the basement to work on his online gift basket company, which he told me was going "very well." By now we hardly saw each other and we were sleeping separately.

While I encouraged the kids to play outside in the mud and take off their shoes and run as fast as they could whenever they could, I had the politest children in America.

"Would you like to go to bed now?" I'd say.

"No, thank you," they'd say.

Not only were my children the first genetic relatives I had ever lived with, but I found them fascinating. I didn't want to spend my nights in comedy clubs. I wanted to spend my time with them while they still wanted to spend time with me, doing really important things. Like digging the mashed banana out from between my laptop keys.

So that's when I thought, *I know. Instead of performing, I'll write a novel with an adopted heroine at its center rather than the usual adopted serial killer—while my kids are sleeping!* So when people ask me why someone from a really happy adoptive family would need to find her birth parents, instead of having to go into the whole story Every Single Time, I could say, "It would take a book to explain. Oh, wait! I've written one!"

Miraculously, *The English American* was published by Simon and Schuster and became a bestseller, so we wouldn't have to worry about money for a very long time. Or so I thought.

Never ever make the mistake of thinking that just because a man knows how to iron, it also means he knows how to handle the family finances.

My kids were seven and nine when I found out that the husband I had married to be safe and because I knew I could trust him not to run off with another woman had lost ALL our money. ALL of it. Not because he was a bad man, but because he didn't know how to do math.

Which, it turns out, is quite important when you're running your own business.

My mother called from England.

"Darling, are you going to leave him?" she said.

"Mum, I made a promise: for better, for worse and all that!"

"Well, Brian made a promise to have and to hold you, but there hasn't been much holding, has there?" Mum said. She'd been horrified when I told her the year before that Brian slept in another room. She went very quiet and then she said, "Your father and I have had a sensational sex life ever since we got married. It's very important, darling." She was seventy at the time.

"I don't think Brian's interested in sex," I'd told Mum.

Bhima is looking at me.

"It was a high price to pay for security," he says.

"Yes," I whisper into his neck. His skin is soft and warm and smells of Bhima. "It was," I say. "But I didn't know that it was possible to be in a really affectionate relationship without fear, so I didn't know what I was missing."

Bhima's arms are wrapped around me now. I love it here.

He's whispering in my ear now, so lightly I can only just catch the words.

"You should have married an Indian who would have fucked you twice a day and given you lots of Indian babies. In my younger days . . ."

CHAPTER 13

We lived on a cul-de-sac on Pine Tree Lane in Morris Plains, New Jersey, for six years, in a stone house with a wishing well outside the front and a bar in the basement. Every Christmas the neighbors would gather with the kids for hot chocolate under a pine tree and wait for Santa to arrive on a fire engine.

At first I thought it was fine.

Then my neighbor's son taught Tom how to shoot a Nerf gun and fire it at the neighbors.

Then I met a teenager who said what she really wanted to do with her life was get a job writing marketing proposals for the pharmaceutical industry.

Then, when I put up an Obama sign on the front lawn, one of the neighbors came up to me and said, "How can you vote for that man? He went to Harvard! He's an elitist!"

"Haha!" I said, laughing uproariously, only later finding out that she wasn't joking.

Then the same neighbor came over to me while we were watching our children playing together and said, "Our pastor told us 9/11 happened because it was God's punishment for Jewish people and Arab people interbreeding."

My kids were still seven and nine and already showing signs of being free-spirited and creative. How could I possibly raise them surrounded by this kind of thinking?

So, in 2010, when I found out that Brian had lost all our money by borrowing against our house and from credit cards without telling me, part of me was in shock and the other part was relieved. To protect the kids, I would have to leave my loveless marriage and figure out a way to raise them elsewhere.

A friend told me about Great Barrington, a small town in the Berkshire Hills of Western Massachusetts: an area that had attracted writers like Edith Wharton and Herman Melville, with a farm-to-table culture—here's the cow, now it's on my plate.

But, my friend said, "Whatever you do, don't go to New England in February."

So I drove up in February, in a snowstorm, and fell instantly in love with the small New England town with a school, a community center, four theaters, Tanglewood—the summer home of the Boston Symphony Orchestra—a co-op, a ski area, a gym, and one department store.

Perfect.

It's the summer of 2010, and I manage to rent an old farmhouse at the end of a mile-long driveway. It's a lovely, wild spot with a stream, a beaver dam, porcupines, bears.

A few days after we move in, the kids are upstairs and I'm sitting on the porch staring at the sky wondering how I'm going to support them, when an enormous moose—yes, a moose—wanders into the garden, stops, turns his head to look me in the eyes for what seems like an age, then saunters majestically towards the stream and disappears into the woods.

"WOW," Bhima says.

"That's what I said." Then, "Bhima?"

"What is it, beautiful woman?"

"Do you think the plural of 'Moose' is 'Meese'?"

"No I don't. You're changing the subject. It can't have been easy, Alison. What did you do for money?"

I couldn't afford to take the time to write another book, which doesn't pay anything until you've spent years writing it, so I knew I'd have to find something else, and fast. And then a miracle happened.

I remember the moment clearly. It was early fall and I was looking out the window at my kids jumping in and out of a huge pile of leaves with their friends outside, not a Nerf gun in sight.

That morning we actually saw a turtle laying eggs outside the kitchen door. Everything was perfect. Except for the fact that we were running out of money.

I remember standing in my kitchen covered in chocolate

chip cookie batter. I hadn't brushed my hair or spoken to anyone over the age of nine in days, when the phone rang.

"Is this Alison Larkin?" a female voice said.

"Used to be," I quipped.

"This is Hillary at Tantor audio. We heard your narration of *The English American* and we know you can do any accent. If you can promise us fifteen audiobooks a year, we'll set you up with a home recording studio so you can earn a living while being a single mom in the middle of the countryside where there's no other work except writing, which you don't seem to be doing much of. Can you do an Australian accent?"

"No problem, mate," I said in an Australian accent.

"How about Scots?"

"Absolootely!" I said, picturing myself narrating sweeping Scottish romances with titles like *Mad, Bad and Dangerous in Plaid.*

"Can you do a Brooklyn male?"

"Why, certainly," I said. Then, in a Brooklyn accent, I said "Go fuck yourself." Then, British again, I said "Which I understand is a colloquialism."

Bhima throws his head back and roars with laughter.

My "recording studio" was set up in the quietest place in the farmhouse, which was my clothes closet—my clothes acting as a most effective sound buffer.

I'd get up at 5:00 a.m., record for two hours, then wake the kids, feed them, and take them to school. I'd come back, record for six more hours, then pick them up from school. Then there'd be laundry. Then there'd be cleaning. Then there'd be cooking. Then I'd collapse into bed. Then another day would begin.

Soon I was recording audiobooks for other publishers, including Blackstone, HarperCollins, Macmillan, and Recorded Books, and in two years I had earned enough money to buy my little house in Stockbridge.

In 2014 someone said, "The publishers are using your name to sell audiobooks. Why don't you set up your own audiobook company and call it Alison Larkin Presents?"

"That was a really good idea," Bhima says.

"It was. I started by narrating *Pride and Prejudice* and

adding songs from Regency England at the end of it. And to my astonishment, it sold. I mean, it really sold! I was homesick for England, so I narrated all of Jane Austen's novels, then *Alice in Wonderland*, then *Jane Eyre*. Then I started hiring other people so I wouldn't have to do all the work. And soon our money problems were over. We were safe. I had found a way to support my kids and raise them in the best way I could think of while doing work I loved.

Bingo.

"You're getting close," Bhima says.

"I am."

"Almost there," he says looking deeply into my eyes.

"Almost."

CHAPTER 14

My kids are almost grown and I'm fifty-three years old. Elizabeth has Darcy, Jane Eyre has Rochester . . . but what about me? It's lonely narrating audiobooks all by yourself in a recording studio.

So I head down to the coffee shop and I start hanging out. There's an older couple there who are really happy together—you can just tell. And then I hear the man has died. And I pluck up the courage to say to the woman, "I've avoided love all my life so I wouldn't have to suffer the way you are now. Was it really worth it?"

And she says, "Yes. Was your choice to avoid love worth it?"

And I say, "I don't know."

At that point I realize that I will never find true love if I don't do something about it before it's too late.

Then a friend says to me, "Why not online date?" Hmmm.

I meet a professor who talks about himself for three hours straight and then tells me what a great conversationalist I am.

I meet a contra dancer who whirls me around so fast and I'm so relieved to be sitting down that I really don't care when I notice he has scrambled egg in his beard. Later, over dinner, he flirts with the waitress, so I just get up and leave.

I speak to a man on the phone who speaks with verrrrry elongated vowel sounds. Within a few minutes he says, "I have millions of dollars in saaaavings and I own a multi-million-dollar company."

"I hope you don't mind my asking," I say politely, "but have you been drinking?"

"Nohhhh," he says. "I'm from Connecticut."

I look at the sky, I say "Please bring me a guy who is cheerful. Who is funny and smart, who has a big heart, who is kind. Bring me a kindred spirit who laughs at the things I do.

Someone I know I really fit with, who I can trust deeply too."

CHAPTER 15

"Now we get to the good part," Bhima says. "Don't leave anything out."

"Okay. But don't interrupt, or I'll lose concentration."

"I promise."

Bhima is lying on the couch with his hands behind his head again, waiting.

My neck's hurting. I know I'm supposed to put my laptop at eye level to stop it from getting worse, but then I won't be able to type as fast as my brain moves, which causes frustration of a different kind. I opt for neck pain.

I'm sitting at Bhima's kitchen table, opposite my favorite Chagall painting of a blue mermaid with orange hair holding a bunch of flowers, floating above the sea.

Remembering Bhima sitting on his couch in Bennington, very still, concentrating on answering a hundred emails, his mind focused on nothing else, I open my laptop and begin writing again.

It's Sunday, January 4, 2019. And the only place you can get a *New York Times* on a Sunday is the Red Lion Inn in Stockbridge. Which is across the road from Austen Riggs, the most famous mental institution in the world, and opposite St Paul's, which is where the artist Norman Rockwell went to church.

Actually, it's where his wife went to church because Norman preferred to sleep in on Sunday mornings. But I digress. Which, by the way, is genetic.

It's a bright sunny day with a blanket of snow on the ground, and I'm heading up the creaky old wooden steps of the Red Lion Inn which was built in 1776, a popular year in the US, less so in

England. I walk past the two red lion statues and onto the porch. And I'm singing in my head:

Bring me someone who gets it,
So I won't want to dash for the exit.

Once inside the inn, I can smell cedar wood. There's a fire and there's a guy at the piano playing lounge music. I walk across the deep red carpet, go over to the reception desk and ask the woman behind the counter for the *New York Times*. She says she's sorry but the last paper's gone. And I say, "Ohhhh. I wanted to do the crossword!"

Then she points to her left and I turn around. And I see this man with curly dark hair about my height, only thinner. And he's looking over at me, holding up the *Sunday Times Magazine*, which has the crossword in it. He's smiling sheepishly at me. And he has the most beautiful eyes.

"I'm sorry, I bought the last paper," he says.

Then he's handing me his *New York Times*.

"No, no. It's okay. I just like to do Sunday's crossword because it's so much easier than Saturday's, which is almost impossible."

"It is," he says.

There's a pause as we look at each other.

"Friday's is hard too," I say.

"Yes."

"They get more difficult as the week goes on."

"They do." Then he takes a step toward me and holds out his hand for me to shake.

"My name is Bhima."

"I'm Alison."

"You sound British."

"You sound Indian."

"South India," he says. "Vizag. Near Hyderabad. Have you been to India?"

"I went to Delhi once, but on my way to Srinagar in Kashmir and Leh in Ladakh."

Bhima is smiling at me.

"Have you been in the US long?" I say.

"Almost thirty years," he says.

"Me too! Why did you come? To America, I mean."

"I came to do a PhD in chemical engineering at RPI when I was twenty-two. Then, after twenty years enduring corporate America, I moved to Vermont."

"A long way from India."

"Indeed. And a completely different culture. My father was an MD in pathology and a college professor. My mother was a schoolteacher. We are Andhra Brahmins with a huge respect for books, knowledge, and wisdom. As kids we cycled through Indian authors and poets but also the English Classics: Charles Dickens, Jane Austen, the Brontës."

"The last time I mentioned the Brontës to an American she thought I was referring to a book about dinosaurs."

Bhima laughs, then he stops. Then he laughs harder. Then he says, "Alison, would you like to go on a walk with me?"

As we walk past the post office and the Elm Street Market and the church on the corner, we pass one of my comedy students.

"Call me!" I say. "I may have a job for you."

"Do you often make job offers to random people on the street?" Bhima asks, laughing again.

"Not so random. I'm in need of an audiobook recording engineer and this kid is a technical whizz, so . . ."

Another voice. A woman's this time. "Alison, how's Lucy?"

This time it's Helga, a wildly talented seventy-nine-year-old Viennese artist who has read *The English American* and comes to all my comedy shows.

"Lucy's well," I say. "I'll tell her I saw you. This is my friend Bhima."

Helga's eyes light up. "You must both come to dinner!" she says.

"No one's used to seeing me with a bloke," I explain to him. "It's usually just me."

Bhima beams.

CHAPTER 16

Half an hour later we're walking along the Mary Flynn Trail in the woods next to the Housatonic River.

The sun is glistening on the snow like diamonds.

"Do you have children?" I ask.

"No," Bhima says.

"Did you want any?"

"My wife and I tried IVF, but no luck."

"So you're married?" I say, my heart sinking.

"Not anymore. We were married for three years. I wanted to travel. She wanted to stay in Albany. We did not make each other happy."

"I'm sorry," I say.

And I am sorry. Just as I am sorry that living with Brian was such an effort.

One of the Bobs rides by on his bike, his wild white hair held down by a maroon beret.

"Hi Alison!"

"Hi Bob," I say, waving back.

"You know everybody," Bhima says. "What are you, the mayor or something? My mom is the same. Everybody knows her, too."

"Where is she?"

"Right now she's in Vizag in India. She has an apartment by the sea. Soon she'll be flying to stay with my sister in California. Then after a few months she'll come to me."

Bhima tells me he wanted to work in renewable energy, so he left corporate America to run a solar power company in Bennington.

"Hang on a second!" I say. "If this is an elaborate ploy to sell me solar panels you're too late. I've already got them."

"Foiled! Damn those other solar guys."

We can't stop laughing. Then, "What about you, Alison? Why did you come to America?"

"I came to find my birth mother . . ."

"Whaaaaat?"

"I was adopted at birth and raised in England and Africa, but when I was twenty-eight I felt a need to find the people I came from, so I came to America and . . . it would take a book to explain. Actually, I've written one. It was based on my one-woman comedy show in which I played my English mother and my American birth mother who was her diametrical opposite in every single way."

I've dropped into a deep Southern accent now and Bhima is roaring with laughter.

"Oh my God! You are so good at accents!"

"It's what I do for a living actually. I can basically do anyone I meet."

I flip into French, Cockney, Irish, Swedish, New Zealand, South African, German, Dutch. We're in the woods, standing next to a tree with thin branches covered with icicles, next to the Housatonic river.

Bhima applauds. There is no one else on the path.

"Can you do my accent?" Bhima says finally.

"Welllll . . ."

"Oh, come on Alison!" he says. "After me. 'The rain in Spain stays mainly in the plain.'"

His eyes are sparkling. And he's quoting *My Fair Lady*. I can't resist. So I don't.

"The rain in Spain stays mainly in the plain," I say, in Bhima's accent.

"Again!"

"The rain in Spain stays mainly in the plain," I say.

"'By George, she's got it!'"

We continue in this vein for the next ten minutes.

And when I am finally allowed to stop, Bhima says, "You must put me in a comedy show one day. But when you do you must promise not to make me sound English or American. Promise me you will do my accent exactly as it is?"

"I promise."

I swear there's laughter of a kind coming from the bushes and trees and wisps of snow floating in the air carried by the wind.

"I would have loved to have been an actor. Did your parents encourage this line of work?"

"When I told my English parents I wanted to be a writer, my Dad—a banker—said, 'Why?' I said, 'Because I like writing.' He said, 'Well, I like playing golf, but I don't delude myself by thinking I can make a living at it.' When I told my American birth mother I wanted to be a writer she said, 'Thank God. 'Cause in our family anyone who even tries an office job gets fired. Our people don't like to be caged.'"

The wind is up.

"You think you had a culture conflict?" Bhima says, "When I arrived in America, I'd never met a Westerner or eaten meat. It was against Hindu tradition, but when I first got here I ate as many hamburgers as I could get my hands on!"

I picture him as he was then. A brave, curious, brilliant twenty-two-year-old arriving in America for the first time, hard working, lonely, speaking very little English, studying for sixteen hours at a time, before heading to the diner for a hamburger, before going back to his room, listening to Coldplay, then falling into bed and starting it all again the next day.

"And I loved the Western way of being free to have sex before marriage," Bhima says. "Although, I swear I should have let my parents arrange a marriage for me. I've had one short American marriage and several American girlfriends, but my GOD American women are so confrontational! It's absolutely exhausting."

"It's the same with American men," I say, thinking of Brian. "Who get particularly irritable when packing."

I look at Bhima who is on a roll.

"In India and England we have a sense of duty," Bhima says. "But in America? It's the 'me-me-me' culture."

"Tell me about it. On the day I flew to America to meet my birth mother, I was sitting next to a woman on the flight who actually said—and I quote word for word—'Hi. I'm Maryanne. I'm an alcoholic, co-dependent, cross-addicted. enabling incest survivor. I'm into yoga, meditation, affirmation, visualization, forgiving, understanding, touching, feeling, asserting, focusing, homecoming, confiding, Buddhism, Hinduism, Creationism, Romanticism, Astrology, Mythology, Erogeny, Intimacy, Mysticism and low fat, low sugar, 'eat-it-and-you-lose-weight' chocolate yoghurt.'"

Bhima is laughing again. "What on earth did you say to that?"

"The only thing I could say. I turned to her and I said, *'Pardonnez-moi madame mais je ne peux pas parler anglais.'*

"Do you play rummy?" I ask suddenly, remembering Charles Wheeler, who was the Washington correspondent for the BBC, and his Sikh wife, Dip, who were great family friends of ours. Dip had the most beautiful long hair, which she wore up most of the time. Right now I'm remembering Dip and her sisters sitting cross-legged on the floor of our cabin on Bryce Mountain in their saris, playing rummy with great passion and glee.

Suddenly Bhima's answer feels very important.

"I do play rummy!" Bhima says. "But I'm not as good as my mother. No one is. She plays for money with her friends and she fleeces them. Would you like to have dinner with me?"

He says it casually.

We can see our breath in the cold winter air.

I'm aware of an extra energy that seems to have come from nowhere.

"On one condition," I say, seriously.

"What's that?"

"You'll agree to play rummy with me over dinner."

I hold my breath. His answer matters. The last person I suggested we play cards with over dinner was an American who took my suggestion as a personal insult, as if it meant I wasn't interested in talking with him, which it didn't mean at all.

"But of course," Bhima says as we head into the Stockbridge General Store where we buy a pack of Women Author playing cards.

The cards are sitting on my bookshelf here, today. They're

next to a picture of Dad and me taken over thirty years ago in England, which in turn is next to Bhima, who is lying on the couch patiently waiting for me to finish writing down everything I remember about the day we met.

"Great start, Alison," Bhima says. "And it was a great day. You were so beautiful and so funny!"

"So you were you."

"I'm distracting you. Didn't we go into the tavern for dinner next?"

CHAPTER 17

We head down the stairs of the Red Lion Inn to the tavern. There's a guy playing jazz at the piano. Chicken pot pie is on the menu, as is red wine.

I take out the cards and start to shuffle. Bhima's eyes are sparkling.

"How about we allow ourselves three questions each?" Bhima says.

"Sure," I say, staring at my cards, not really concentrating.

"Okay," Bhima begins. "What do you really want, Alison?"

"Apart from to win this game of rummy?"

"Ha! Yes. Apart from that."

"You were always so happy when you won Rummy, Alison," Bhima says, laughing, from the couch.

"It's true," I say. I don't know why I can't stop grinning when I win at cards, but I really can't.

I stop typing and look over at him suspiciously.

"Wait a second. Did you ever let me win?"

"*Moi?*" Bhima says, his face a picture of innocence.

I stop typing.

"Did you?" I ask.

"Would I?"

"You might."

Back in 2019, the wildly attractive Indian gentleman I've just met has just asked me what I really want. And he deserves an answer.

"I want to live a life I love," I say simply. "I don't want to just get through the rest of my life. I want to really live it."

"I see," Bhima says, picking up the ten of clubs that I have just laid down. "So, name me something that would help you do that."

"Well, I want to keep doing work that leaves the world a bit better than when I found it."

He's looking at me intently.

"What else?"

"And now that my children are grown up, I want to reconnect with old friends."

"And?"

"I want to travel again."

He looks slightly disappointed, but there is no way I'm going to tell a man I only met three hours ago, who feels utterly familiar to me, that I want to find love. True love. The kind I have longed for all my life but have not yet managed to find.

I put down an ace of diamonds.

"Your turn now," I say. "What is it YOU want?"

"First, I want to find a woman to love, so I am not alone." Bhima says.

Damn. "And?"

"I want to travel," he says, smiling.

"And?"

"I want to figure out how to turn plastics into fuel."

A moment passes. If not now, when?

"There is one other thing I want," I say.

"And what is that?"

"I want to find the kind of love that really fits. With chemistry. For example, I am sure I can't be with someone with whom there is no chemistry, no matter how well I get on with them. Neither could I be happy with someone I didn't get on with, no matter how great the chemistry."

"I see."

I win the game of rummy.

We're still in the tavern half an hour and a bottle of red wine later.

"So you, a transplanted Briton, and I, an Indian, are stuck here in this benighted country," Bhima says.

"Yes."

"Having lived here these thirty-odd years, I suppose this is home. Even though I refuse to give up my Indian accent, there's a lot to love here: basketball, jazz, the beauty of nature. And then, some part of me continues to long for India."

"Some part of me continues to long for England."

"But the India I miss is long gone."

"But the England I miss is long gone. Although I didn't really grow up there. We lived in East and West Africa and we had friends from India and . . ."

I don't drink for a reason. It goes straight to my head. I'm feeling relaxed for the first time in eons.

The candles on the tables are flickering in the evening light.

CHAPTER 18

"Alison," Bhima says suddenly, "have you ever loved a person of color?"

"Two."

"Who?"

"Aloysius, at college."

"Where was he from?"

"Sri Lanka."

"I hate him already. And who was the second?"

"Archbishop Desmond Tutu."

"Damn, I love him too."

Then I told him the story of how I met Desmond Tutu.

Bhima and I are in the lobby a bit later when a woman says to Bhima, "If you and your wife want to sit by the fire, we're just leaving."

With a completely straight face Bhima says, "My wife and I are very grateful," and we sit down on the small velvet sofa opposite the fire. Then he picks up the crossword again and says, "I could use some help with three across."

We're in a bubble, surrounded by an extra energy and a kind of peace. He's looking at the crossword saying nothing.

Finally I say, "What's the clue?" Bhima lifts his head and looks me in the eyes and says, "Sound of a lightning bolt. Three letters. Middle letter, A."

And we both say, "ZAP!"

CHAPTER 19

January 6, 2019

Subject: Meeting you

Alison! What a wonderful afternoon and evening. Where do I start? First, we can get the awkward stuff out of the way. I am so sorry about the kiss. Sigh!

January 6, 2019

Subject: RE: Meeting you

It was my fault for turning my head at the last second. It was quite interesting, actually. I don't think I've ever been kissed on the eyebrow before.

January 6, 2019

Subject: RE: Meeting You

I so thoroughly enjoyed being with you, your sense of humor and your joie de vivre! I know chemistry is important to you. Do you believe you could know right away if there is chemistry? I would love to see you again and look forward to hearing from you. Have a great weekend.

January 6, 2019

Subject: RE: Meeting You

Good morning Bhima! I would love to see you again too. To answer your question re chemistry, I think you

can know right away if you absolutely don't find someone attractive, i.e. if you will never—ever—ever want
to kiss them, because of the way they smell, or because you just flat out don't fancy them. But if there
is connection and liking and compatibility and neither of you looks like the back end of a bus and there's
something there—you're not sure what, but it's something—well, then I think there's a chance chemistry
will develop over time.

"Wait a second, Alison" Bhima says from the couch. "Did
you keep all my emails?"
"Every single one."
"Me too."
"And I kept your two poems," I say.
"Oh God. My poems. Are you going to put them in this
book?"
"Not sure yet. But I am going to read through your emails
because that way I can be sure to quote you in your own words."
"Fair enough. Carry on."

January 6, 2019

Subject: RE: Meeting You

Something I didn't tell you when we met—I had a triple bypass surgery in 2015. It was completely unex-
pected. I started experiencing chest pains, went in to
have it checked out, and discovered three blocked ar-
teries and an aneurysm. The surgery went well but it
took me a year to recover.
A year later, my marriage ended. It had become a long
distance thing with my wife spending the majority of
her time in Albany and me in Bennington. I battled
other health problems.
In 2018 I foolishly entered into an even longer distance relationship. But she had no intention of moving and my business is in Vermont so we couldn't
come up with a plan for long-term togetherness.
Enter 2019 and I unexpectedly meet a lovely,

wonderful, talented woman, a.k.a. you, with whom I have so much in common. But I am now thinking that the next lady I become involved with should be someone close-by already or who would come and live with me. Would you consider that, do you think? I am not sure I can go through the heartbreak of another long-distance relationship. I would love to hear your thoughts on whether or not you would be interested in something like this.

January 6, 2019

Subject: RE: Meeting You

Are you always this direct? I love it. I'm not interested in a long-distance relationship either. But I do think it is a good idea to meet someone more than once before deciding whether or not to live with them.

January 6, 2019

Subject: RE: Meeting You

So there is hope?

January 6, 2019

Subject: RE: Meeting You

There is.

January 6, 2019

Subject: RE: Meeting You

Would you like to get together again?

January 6, 2019

Subject: RE: Meeting You

When?

January 6, 2019

Subject: RE: Meeting You

Would tomorrow be too soon?

"I was already in love with you, you know," Bhima says.
"Were you really?"
"Oh, yes."
"It took me a bit longer."
"I know," Bhima says.

CHAPTER 20

We meet for the second time in Williamstown and go to see a Korean film. I fall asleep, because it's been a long week. Bhima doesn't notice, fortunately, or if he does, he doesn't say anything.

"Did you notice?" I ask Bhima. "Or don't you remember?"

"Oh, I remember everything. And yes, I did notice. But your head rested on my shoulder so I didn't mind. Concentrate on writing down the story, Alison."

"Alright."

After the movie, Bhima and I go to the Blue Mango Thai and Japanese restaurant on Spring Street for dinner and sit by the window. Bhima orders lo mein. I'm fascinated by what Bhima has to say about climate change and he tells me more about his plan to turn plastics into fuel.

"Have you thought of giving lectures?" I say.

"If I could find a way to make a living at the same time as giving lectures, I would."

He's looking at me. I'm remembering the kiss.

I have never kissed on what turned out to be a first date before and—well, he missed. I mean he really did miss. And that could be a problem.

"I think we have a lot in common," I say suddenly, "but if there is no chemistry then let's not date. Let's just be friends."

"Okay," Bhima says, tucking into his noodles.

"But," I say, tucking in to mine, "if there IS chemistry, shall we date?"

"Sure thing."

We're opposite the cinema and a red brick building on stilts, which houses apartments and Pappa Charlie's Deli. About two hundred yards farther down is Tunnel City Coffee, the coffee shop where the Williams College students hang out.

We share a Thai donut for dessert, split the bill, and leave the restaurant.

"So when do you propose we test the chemistry, Alison?" Bhima says.

"I'm not sure."

"Perhaps we should try kissing again today?" he says.

"Okay," I say. "But properly this time. Try not to miss . . ."

"I will do my best."

Bhima takes my hand and crosses the street toward the red brick building. It's cold and dark and while there are one or two cars driving past and a student or two, we're basically alone.

Bhima is wearing a black winter jacket, and I am in my light green parka.

Bhima has a confidence about him that I find as attractive as his face. He's not conventionally handsome. He's more interesting than that. A year ago, my friend Annette called him "luminous." If I had to use just one word to describe him, that would be it, I think.

Bhima puts his hands on either side of my face as he kisses me properly for the first time. And within seconds we're lost.

"What do you think?" Bhima says five minutes later.

"About what?"

"The chemistry."

"Well you did get a PhD in chemical engineering."

We're both grinning. Then we're laughing so hard we're crying.

Then Bhima takes my arm, leads me back toward my car, and kisses me goodbye.

And we're off.

CHAPTER 21

January 17, 2019

Bhima Nitta: Good morning Alison! Where are you today?

Alison Larkin: In the Kripalu café, writing.

Bhima Nitta: Kripalu?

Alison Larkin: It's a Hindu retreat in the Berkshire Hills where overloaded people from New York go to do yoga and meditate and take workshops.

Bhima Nitta: You're not Hindu are you?

Alison Larkin: Ha. No. I go there for lunch. And because they sell these delicious chocolate peanut butter cups which I like very much.

Bhima Nitta: I see.

Alison Larkin: Plus there's a sunroom on the fourth floor with the comfiest seats in the world and huge glass windows out of which you can see the lake and mountains and blue, blue sky. Are you Hindu?

Bhima Nitta: No. I'm an atheist. My parents are, though. I left it all behind when I left India. They're cults mostly that exist to get as much money out of people as possible.

Alison Larkin: I guess all organized religions are, if you think about them that way.

✳ ✳ ✳

January 18, 2019
8 p.m.

Bhima Nitta: For dinner I heated up some week-old lentil soup (broccoli dal), made some rice and called it good. In reality it was only borderline edible. How about you?
Alison Larkin: I appear to be having cereal for dinner.
Bhima Nitta: You eat so much better when you are with me.
Alison Larkin: I do.

January 19, 2019
7 p.m.

Alison Larkin: Why, out of all the Hindi movies you could have suggested I watch, did you choose *The Lunchbox*?
Bhima Nitta: Did you like it?
Alison Larkin: I loved it. It resonated.
Bhima Nitta: How so, Ms. Larkin?
Alison Larkin: Well, it's a film about a woman who longs to connect romantically with her husband, who has very little interest in her. And its message seems to be that if you are in a lonely, miserable marriage full of nothing but hard work and chores, it is not only okay, but imperative to stay open to the possibility of finding True Love elsewhere.
Bhima Nitta: Have you ever experienced True Love?
Alison Larkin: Not yet. The fit has never been right.
Bhima Nitta: Same. But I've seen it in the movies. *The Princess Bride* is my absolute favorite movie. Not only is it hilarious but it has a lot about true love in it.

❋ ❋ ❋

January 20, 2019

Alison Larkin: While it is true that we have known each other for almost 7 days, 13 hours of which we have spent in each other's company, you have spent many hours reading my autobiographical novel and I have only been able to watch one film that you like. That is hardly equal footing!

Yours, in complaint, Alison

Bhima Nitta: Hahaha! I agree. More movie picks for you. Here's another one—*Lion*. This one (made in 2016, partly in India) you may especially relate to, for reasons I leave you to discover . . .

Alison Larkin: I have already seen *Lion*, so you must come up with more.

Bhima Nitta: *Monsoon Wedding*

Drishyam (slow burn thriller)

Kahaani (woman-power action)

Delhi Belly (it's a laugh riot)

Alison Larkin: I will watch these forthwith.

Bhima Nitta: I can't put your book down and I can't wait to see you tomorrow. Let's meet at the Southern Vermont Coffee Shop. Then we can go for a hike, Scrabble, lunch, tea, and a walk to a historic house near where I live . . . I'll be waiting, with bells on!

P.S. I can't believe you're even giving me the time of day.

CHAPTER 22

Ican't believe I've met someone who I just flat out love to be with. So I do give him the time of day. And in time I give him my nights. And soon we are wearing the road out between Stockbridge, Massachusetts, and Bennington, Vermont, which are just over an hour apart, depending on how fast you drive.

Bhima lives in a house powered by sustainable energy in the heart of a forty-acre wood. Often, when I come to see him, I have to stop to let a family of deer cross the long dirt driveway that leads to his house.

Bhima refuses to allow hunting on his land, and as a result all kinds of wildlife have found refuge there. Hawks fly overhead in the winter, hummingbirds stop by in the summer, and the view from the top of the woods reminds me so much of England that I get a lump in my throat whenever I look out over the fields and little country roads below.

✳ ✳ ✳

"I realized I had found the woman I was looking for on our first walk behind the McCullough house in North Bennington," Bhima says suddenly.

He's been reading over my shoulder.

"Really?" I stop typing and look at him.

"Yes. There was that old stone building—sort of like a mini ruin, if I remember correctly."

"Yes."

"You took to it as if it were a stage and you sang 'Wouldn't It Be Lovely?' from *My Fair Lady*. And I knew that was it. We must have watched it on TV in India a dozen times when we were kids."

"Us too. When we lived in Kenya."

"Why don't you put on some music while you're writing?" Bhima says.

"How about some Arijit Singh?" I say.

"How about 'Wouldn't It Be Loverly?'" Bhima says.

I head over to the speakers my friend Bob brought me from the thrift shop, find the song on my iPhone, and press play.

And Bhima and I sit listening to the music, remembering that cold snowy day in Bennington, Vermont, as if it were yesterday.

❆ ❆ ❆

Soon after we meet, we realize that Bhima is the only Indian guy in his community and I'm the only Brit in mine, and in a small town news travels fast.

"Let's give them something to talk about," Bhima says. And we do.

"You're the only person of color here!" I say.

"Always am," Bhima says proudly.

We're holding hands as we head into Monument Mountain High School to watch my daughter in a play.

There's something comforting about sitting next to someone else who finds the All-American high school atmosphere with moms selling Fritos and M&Ms and lemonade before the show as alien as I do.

I've seen dozens of concerts and plays in this auditorium. Even though the slight smell of stale feet is still very much there, with Bhima at my side I feel alert and present as we watch Lucy playing Malvolio in *Twelfth Night*, brilliantly.

"Your kids are so talented," Bhima says.

"They are," I say proudly. "And they're curious and thought-ful, too. Tom asked me recently why anyone gets upset—ever—if a boy falls in love with a boy or a girl with a girl. He just didn't get why it's such a big deal to some people."

"What did you say?"

"I said the reason this kind of stupidity exists is because we live in a patriarchal society. And we have done for hundreds of years. So to demonstrate this, I thought, 'Why don't I take one of the most famous books in English literature and change the gender of the protagonist?'"

"What did you pick?"

"*Great Expectations!*"

"That's my favorite book!"

"Only in this version I turned Pip into a girl."

"*Merde alors!*"

"I was interested to see if changing Pip's gender would change the way I felt when I heard the story."

"And did it?"

"Nope. It changed nothing. Except it suddenly became normal for a girl to learn to read, or for a girl to kiss a girl, or for a girl to walk into a bar without being molested. Which of course never happened in the nineteenth century. I'm not sure if we'll sell any audiobooks, but—hey."

"Fascinating."

"I'm glad you think so, Mr. Nitta."

"I do, Ms. Larkin. How about you do the same with Scrooge?"

"Good idea. Will do."

CHAPTER 23

One Saturday we're walking through the woods leading to the house where Robert Frost lived, and we pass a woman who stops, looks at us, and says, "Oh my god! You two are so in love!"

We wait until she has passed us by, then we turn to each other and say, "Only in America."

"We can't be in love," I say.

"Why not?" Bhima says.

"There's no friction. We don't have to negotiate."

"I know," Bhima says. "Isn't it great?"

Bhima is extra motivated to be healthy because of the triple bypass which saved his life five years earlier.

He also tells me that his arm is full of steel due to a motor-cycle accident in his twenties and that he almost died when he was thirty, racing cars at Lime Rock. But his cardiologist has told him that if he keeps exercising and stays stress-free and healthy, his heart will last as long as anybody else's. And I tell him I think the steel in his arm is kind of cool.

I realize I'm toast on one of our long winter hikes up Mount Greylock on about our ninth date. We're walking up a steep path. I follow behind Bhima, who is wearing black nylon pants, his gray flannel tartan jacket, and a pair of hiking boots. As we get higher, there is ice on the ground and I'm suddenly slipping all over the place.

"Alison, what are you wearing on your feet? Those are summer sneakers that are falling apart. It's not safe!"

Then Bhima sits down in the snow, takes off his hiking boots, and insists I put them on my feet. And soon I am scampering down the mountain in his hiking boots and he is scampering down the mountain in my motley old sneakers.

"I don't think I was scampering," Bhima says as he reads. "More like skidding."

"Stop interrupting."

"Ok, ok."

Bhima has this look. He'll look at my kitchen knives and say, "Alison, these knives are blunt. In your house it is actually dangerous to cut a carrot."

The next weekend a knife sharpener arrived. With a pair of hiking boots.

※　※　※

Instead of pulling away I allow myself to come closer.

I almost walk away of course. But only once.

It happens at a library fundraising event in North Bennington. Bhima tells me I'm going to meet all the people in his community, including his ex-girlfriend Nicole with whom he is still friends.

In the library there is cheese and wine and there are maybe twenty people milling about. Six-foot-five Vermonters keep coming up to Bhima, who is five-foot-six, and bashing him on the back and saying, "Thanks for getting us into community solar, our electric bill is waaaaaaay down." And Bhima beams.

Then I see this incredibly beautiful and very thin woman who would make Margot Robbie look ordinary and I think, *There's Nicole*. And I make myself go over to this goddess and I say, "Hallo, I'm Alison."

"Hallo. I'm Nicky." Her voice is deep and sultry.

"What is it that you do?"

"I'm a waitress."

My adrenaline is running and I'm about to simply walk out, when out of the corner of my eye I see Bhima coming over with a perfectly nice, ordinary woman about my size, who is smiling at me.

"Alison, this is Nicole," Bhima says.

"Oh, hallo!" I say. "HALLO!"

And as she tells me about her life, I realize I like Nicole a lot and I know we'll be friends. And Bhima's eyes are sparkling as he watches us from the other side of the room talking for over an hour.

And later, because somehow he understands without my having told him anything, Bhima walks over to me and puts his mouth close to my ear and whispers, "Alison, I want only you."

And when Bhima gets jealous because I'm working on an audiobook with a particularly good-looking actor, I make a point of saying "by the way, Bhima, he's gay."

"Wonderful!"

CHAPTER 24

When we're not together we're texting each other or we're on the phone.

"I just had a surprising call from the mammogram people, who want me to go in so they can take additional images of my left breast," I tell Bhima one day.

"Your left breast is a thing of beauty. I will not take kindly to people who cast aspersions on it!"

"I shall tell them if they make any more rude remarks they'll have to look out for a cross Indian gentleman jumping to my defense. I was thinking of skipping the appointment altogether, but I suppose I should go and do my part towards keeping the radiologists in employment. Wait. I'm okay. I just got a text from the mammogram people. Everything's fine."

"Bastards. I'll call you later."

* * *

One day I decide to get a didgeridoo, which Bhima finds hilarious.

"You should get one too," I say. "Then we can set up a double act."

"I'll be Didgeri and you can be Doo!" Bhima says. "We'll set up three-hour-long concerts in Vermont and Massachusetts and make everyone we know come and listen to us. And they'll have to come because we'll be the only interracial didgeridoo couple in New England and they won't want to appear racist."

We find this very, very amusing.

"Why is it that so few Americans have a sense of humor?"

"I have a theory," Bhima says. "America is still an empire.

Apart from the satirical, post-ironic crowd, most Americans still think they live in the best country on Earth.

"The English, on the other hand, having colonized half the world and, having been driven out of the very same half by the people they colonized, have learned a thing or two about hubris and have become sadder and wiser. And funnier as a result, when they reflect on the absurdity of it all—and the absurd in general. Just a theory . . ."

"I'm sure you're right."

* * *

The main reason I don't perform comedy as much as I used to is because I like to go to bed early so I can get up at sunrise. But Lisa Cavender, who designs my audiobook covers, asked me very nicely if I would help the Literacy Network with their annual gala fundraiser, which was happening in the late afternoon, so I said yes.

"You're doing comedy AND being the auctioneer?" Bhima says.

"You coming?"

"I'll be out there with bells on!" Bhima says.

"There will be press. We'll be photographed."

"I'll wear my suit."

* * *

"You were wonderful, baby. So funny. I loved it! My favorite part was when you took your shoes off and decided to do the whole thing from the top of the chair so people could see you. And you raised $28,000 just by asking for it!" Bhima says.

"Did you see the photo of us in the paper?"

"I did. We look great."

"We do."

"Usually, after performances, I feel depleted. But with you there I could have stayed for hours. Thank you for coming."

"I wouldn't have missed it for the world."

CHAPTER 25

"Are you going to help me make the bed?" I say to him one day.

"I don't make beds. I'm a Brahman," he says.

"Very funny," I say.

He looks up from his iPhone with a puzzled expression.

How fascinating. Surely Bhima knows me well enough by now to know that I am not going to spend my precious time on this Earth washing his sheets, cooking his meals, cleaning his house, or making his bed.

"Did you really say that?" I ask, incredulous.

"I did," he says.

I'm laughing now.

"Ohhhhhhhh, Bhima, no. If you want someone to do all that, you must find them. But it's not going to be me."

He looks a bit surprised, thinks for a moment, then says, "I do want to be with you, so sacrifices must be made."

I hand him the other side of his yellow and gold duvet from India, and after smoothing the sheets, we pull it up over the bed together.

And from that point on, if I go downstairs to make coffee in the mornings, he will make the bed. Or if he goes downstairs to make coffee, I will.

And then whoever did not make the bed that day will exclaim in surprise when they see the bed and say, "Thank you so much for making the bed" to the other, in a very British sort of way.

And there is equality in the household chores from that moment on.

＊ ＊ ＊

With the exception of myself, Bhima prefers plants and animals to people. I asked him if he ever felt lonely living in the middle of the woods before he met me and he said, "Why would I be lonely? We humans are just one of a billion species. I'm surrounded by trees and animals and birds and plants."

If we're out walking in a field, past rivers and trees, and we see a couple with a beautiful baby and someone walking a dog he'll say, "Look at the cute little doggy!"

Then, "Look Alison! That's a red-tailed hawk! Look how it's being harassed by the sparrows that are so much smaller than it is!"

And I do look. I really look. And, I begin to see the natural world through his eyes.

When Bhima tells me he's stressed at work, I suggest he do the work only he can do and delegate the rest. And he does.

We're both running our companies and we both work incredibly hard with intense focus.

But Bhima knows how to stop working after 5:00 p.m. and at the weekends. And I, who have not taken a day off in years, stop working when he does and begin to breathe again.

On Saturdays we go to the Bennington tennis clinic, then we go to Bhima's house and eat lunch and play rummy while we listen to jazz.

Bhima insists we exercise every day. Why? Because before I met him, Bhima became a devotee of a book called *Younger Next Year*. The idea behind this book is that if you work out every single day—I mean really work out, not just phone it in—the cells in your body will recycle and regenerate, so your body will literally be younger the next year. Bhima has been lifting weights while watching every pound.

"Alison! Do you think I have built muscle?"

One day through his bathroom door I actually hear, "Oh, my God Alison! I weigh 133 pounds! I'm obese!"

＊ ＊ ＊

"Are you afraid of death?" I ask Bhima one day.

"Not at all."

"Me neither."

We're lying next to each other on Bhima's bed. It's almost spring. Most of the trees are still bare, but the sunlight on the snow is brighter and the days are starting to get longer.

"I remember when I had my triple bypass surgery," Bhima says. "It was all very sudden. I had chest pains and my wife insisted I go to the hospital and the doctor said if they did not do the surgery right away, I'd be dead. I remember not really caring if I lived or died. It was quite interesting, actually."

"Were you glad you were alive when you came round?"

"Sure," he says, with a half-shrug. "But I am definitely glad now. Because . . ." he says, turning toward me.

"Because?"

"Because if I had died, I would not have known what it was like to love you."

I lie under his yellow duvet, holding his hand lightly, taking this in.

CHAPTER 26

Everything changes when you fall in love, doesn't it? When a writer/comic who knows zip about science falls in love with someone with a PhD in chemical engineering, well, she gets an education.

I want to know Bhima, so I listen to him talking about the things he's interested in for hours. Like why it's so vital we do everything we can to combat climate change.

Up until then I didn't know much about climate change. I mean, I knew it was happening, obviously. But I had no idea how serious the situation was until I met Bhima.

Bhima would walk around the house in his light green lungi reading the news on his iPhone—he refused to have a TV—and when he read the news his body would become very tense. He was horrified by what was going on in Washington.

And he was especially horrified by the deliberate undermining of trust in science. He'd ask me to read the paper to him sometimes.

"Oh, no," I say one day. "You're not going to like this."

"Read it to me anyway."

"'Climate change is a liberal conspiracy put about by corrupt scientists.' And . . . oh, no."

"What?"

"'Fossil fuels are given to us by God and when we burn them it is a blessing on the world,'" I read.

"Existential threats are coming to us all," Bhima says. Quiet. Tense. Furious. "They should be dealt with by us all. How can they be so utterly stupid?"

Bhima knows we're in trouble and I want to soothe him, so

I make it my mission to find ways to bring him joy in the midst of the political and environmental madness that seems to be worsening every day.

"It's not all on your shoulders you know, Bhima," I say. I've been rubbing his back in candlelight after making love for hours. "There's another generation coming. My son marched against climate change in New York. My daughter's on the case too."

"Well, if your kids are on the case," Bhima says. Then, after a long moment he looks at me seriously and says, "It seems I have a choice: I can look at the facts and be depressed, or try not to think about the facts all the time and let myself fall more deeply in love. Let's go to back to bed."

CHAPTER 27

We sleep wrapped up in each other's arms all night long. And every morning, when we wake, Bhima says, "Hello, beautiful woman."

And once trust has built, love builds. It's like wearing a pair of shoes that are too tight for your entire life then finally taking them off.

Here we both are in our fifties, fully in love for the first time in our lives with someone who gets us. And I know in my knower that this is a man I can trust with my life—and who won't be irritable when packing.

At long last, I'm not only in love, I'm also at peace.

"Bhima?"

"What is it, beautiful woman?"

"If you were going to die in a year, what would you do with your time?"

"I am not going to die in a year!"

"I know, I know. But if you were. What are your three favorite things? Don't think, just say the first things that come into your head."

"Cricket, the Costa Brava, and car racing."

My parents live in Chichester, near the Festival of Speed (car racing.) And there are cricket matches at Lord's in London. And my best friend has an old stone house she's looking to rent on the Costa Brava.

Two months later we're on our way.

Anyone can have fun on vacation. But we've each found the person with whom we can have as much fun on the flight on the way over.

In between flights, to make sure we stick to Bhima's rigorous exercise schedule, we run from one end of the airport to the other at top speed, trying not to bump into people's luggage, but when we do saying, "So sorry, we're late for our flight." Then, when we get as far as we can go, we look at each other like bad actors and go, "Oh, no! Wrong terminal!"

Then we run to the next terminal, until Bhima deems we have worked out enough for the day.

※   ※   ※

Bhima went to a cricket match at Lord's, and we both went to the Costa Brava and then we went to Chichester to stay with my parents.

We arrived in the morning and the first thing my eighty-eight-year-old Mum said was, "Welcome Bhima! Would you like some toast and marmalade?"

And then Dad put his hand on Bhima's shoulder and said, "I'm terribly sorry about what we did to India."

I watch Bhima restrain a yelp of laughter, turn to my father politely and say, "It's alright, Rob, it wasn't your fault. At least we got a good education out of it." And then, to me, in a delighted whisper, "Oh, my god, Alison, I LOVE your parents!"

Bhima goes to see the car racing at the Festival of Speed in the morning and returns at four o'clock.

Dad is sitting on the sofa, opposite the painting my youngest brother painted for them of Trumley, the two old flint cottages turned into a house that became our home at the foot of the South Downs and in which they'd lived so happily for more than forty years.

When Bhima arrives home, Dad's eyes light up.

"AH! Bhima! Would you like to see some photographs?" Before Bhima can reply, Dad places the first of several large photo albums on Bhima's lap.

Dad shows Bhima the photographs he's compiled meticulously over the years, dated correctly with details of exactly when each photograph was taken and the names of everyone in it.

In this way, Bhima sees our family growing up in America, Kenya and the Ivory Coast in West Africa, pictures of my brothers

and me crossing rope bridges, camping in the Serengeti game
park, skiing in France, climbing mountains in the Lake District.

Then Dad opens his favorite album. The one he opens at
least once a week.

It's full of pictures of Mum.

Mum with Dad, Mum with us, Mum when she was a beautiful young woman looking like a 1950s model, Mum as an older
woman on top of a mountain after a long hike with our black
labrador Nicky by her side. Mum now holding Dad's hand in the
garden.

"Isn't she beautiful, Bhima?" Dad says.

"Yes!" Bhima says, smiling at me and Mum at the same time.

"Isn't she beautiful, Ali?"

"Yes, Dad," I say. "She's beautiful!"

"What?

"YES DAD!" I have to shout and over-articulate because
he's so hard of hearing.

"There's no need to shout, darling," Mum says from the
kitchen, bringing Bhima another cup of tea and some ginger cake.

"Do you play rummy, Bhima?" Mum says a little later.

"Yes," Bhima says.

"What about Totopoly or Rummikub?" Dad says.

"Ummm . . ."

"Buccaneer? No? How about Stratego? No? Not to worry,"
Dad says, slapping Bhima on the back. "We'll teach you!"

* * *

Still later, after watching the cricket, Bhima and I are sitting
on the sofa reading *The Times* and Dad's reading through his
emails while Mum putters about in the kitchen.

"Another one bites the dust," Dad says suddenly, referring
to yet another of his friends who's just died.

"Who is it this time?" Mum says.

"Rita Wass." Dad looks over at Mum, confused. "Didn't we
already go to her funeral?"

"That was their daughter, Rachel."

"What?"

Dad's father went deaf and so did his father before him, and despite advanced hearing aids and frequent visits to London to see Dr. Gooligong the audiologist, there's little that can be done. But when Mum sits directly in front of Dad and speaks loudly and clearly, he can usually understand quite well. She does this now.

"Rachel Wass died of cancer last year," Mum says loudly.

"Ah yes. Rachel. Pretty girl. Married that strange-looking fellow who was shaped like a pear."

Bhima looks at me for a nanosecond and then quickly looks away in a failed attempt to keep us both from laughing.

Dad doesn't hear Mum's reply because she has left the sitting room for the kitchen.

Next to the bread bin and the kettle is the kitchen window through which she can see the spire of Chichester Cathedral standing tall above the buildings that have housed the people of Chichester for hundreds of years.

"Memorial or funeral?" Mum calls from the other room.

"Funeral, I'm afraid."

"Oh, dear. Well, it'll be fun to see the family again. I'll put it in the diary."

I take a bite out of the remains of the ginger cake, marveling, not for the first time, at how moist it is. You can't get cake like this in America. Unless it's the vegan orange cake they sell at Guido's in Pittsfield, Massachusetts, which is almost as moist as Kipling's ginger cake, but not quite.

Dad turns to us abruptly and says, "Did you know that's the fourth friend of ours who's kicked the bucket this year?"

Our mouths are full of cake, so Bhima and I shake our heads "no."

"Ah, well," Dad says.

"Why don't you three go on a walk to Kingley Vale?" Mum says. "I can pick you up at the pub."

And thus it is that Bhima, my octogenarian father, and I head out for a walk on the South Downs.

Dad in his safari hat, Bhima in his orange-checked shirt and me in jeans and a white T-shirt walk five miles up Kingley Vale, from where we can see Goodwood where the cars are still racing far below.

Bhima is kindness itself to Dad, who shouts at him happily through the wind as we walk and quickly gives up on trying to hear anything either of us are saying. Bhima stands on top of a pile of rocks and Dad takes a picture. We walk for about three hours until we get to the pub where Mum comes to pick us up.

At one point, after our walk, while we're sitting under the awning at the Frog and Thistle drinking a beer, Mum takes Bhima's hand and says, "We've never seen Alison so happy, Bhima. Thank you."

Moved, Bhima replies, "My family say the same to me. So, thank YOU."

The next morning, as Bhima is pulling out of the garage, Dad shouts, "Make sure you don't run over my golf clubs!" Then, after a pause, he shouts, "On second thought, please do. I'm fed up with golf. I've had enough of it."

"Bhima is absolutely wonderful!" Mum says to me as we're leaving.

"And he doesn't do all that connecty-connecty emotional stuff the Americans are so fond of," my father shouts.

"Oh, I think he does, just not in words," Mum says.

Bhima and I quote Dad's "I'm terribly sorry about what we did to India" line for weeks afterwards.

CHAPTER 28

"Sing the duet for me, Alison!" Bhima says now, here, today, over two years since he died.

"Mum and Dad's duet?"

"Yes! From *Grief . . . A Comedy.*"

Bhima is referring to the one-person show I mentioned in the prologue to this book. The one Archbishop Desmond Tutu asked me to write. The one about Bhima and me.

"I love that song!" Bhima says again. "I'll sit on the couch as if I'm the audience. You be your parents, singing the duet. Then do the rest of the show for me. Or at least some of it!"

"Alright, alright," I say, unable to resist the request.

And I begin to sing.

MUM: As any parent here can tell
When your child is doing well
You sleep better.

DAD: When your children are in trouble or sad
Then you're sad, too.

MUM: So when your daughter in America
Who's had a tricky time
After years of causing worry
Finds the true love of her life

DAD: It's cause for celebration
Over here in the UK.
The moment we met Bhima
All our worry went away.

MUM: We've never seen her so happy
Thanks to this new chappie
Bhima from South India.

DAD: He is charming and funny
And jolly good at rummy
And absolutely perfect for her!

MUM: When we lived Africa
She met people from all countries,
From Australia and China and Nepal.

DAD: She grew up with friends from Kenya
And Hong Kong and Abyssinia
Then married a man who'd never travelled at all!

MUM: But everything's alright
Now she's with Bhima.
He likes cricket and tennis
And doing crosswords

DAD: He's read Dickens and Shakespeare
And damn, I really like him,
On our walk he even knew the names of local birds.

MUM: You can tell that he loves everything about her.

DAD: Which is surprising because she can actually be very annoying. Do you think he plays bridge? I wouldn't be surprised because, like me, he's very good at maths!

MUM: She's had a challenging time
In the US of A
Now they're talking of moving
To England one day!

DAD: We've never seen her so happy
It's such a relief

We're happy she's happy
Our job is complete.

Bhima claps as I finish the song. And I bow.

"Now, Alison, finish writing the rest of the story about what happened between us while I was still alive so you can get to the really exciting part, i.e. what happened afterwards."

CHAPTER 29

Soon, I have visited Bhima's mother and brothers and sister, who moved to the United States from India soon after Bhima did. They remind me of my own family: riotous games of rummy around a big wooden table, family meals, laughter, and love. But instead of toast and marmalade, thanks to Bhima's mother, who is an outstanding cook, we have idli with sambar and coconut chutney. For breakfast!

Bhima shared a text from his brother after I first met his family that said, "Alison's great. Don't fuck it up."

❋ ❋ ❋

When Bhima tried to swim, he sank, so he wears arm bands and an orange vest that keep him afloat. And after a short time he's joining me in my favorite summer activity of floating on my back in the middle of a lake looking up at the sky.

Soon, this serious scientist has gone from being mostly tense to mostly relaxed.

A year and a half into our relationship Bhima has even started injecting jokes into his renewable energy presentations.

"What is a solar panel's favorite song?" Bhima says during a speech at a conference. 'Don't Let the Sun Go Down on Me.'"

Out of Bhima's bedroom window we watch the green leaves turn yellow, then red, then brilliant orange, then fall to the ground.

Once, he saves my life. We're out walking near the farmer's market and suddenly there's a fierce wind and a tent lifts up off the ground and one of the poles from the tent is crashing toward my head. Bhima yanks me out of the way just in time.

That night we begin to talk about spending the rest of our lives together.

"We must have a dog," Bhima pronounces.

"A dachshund!" I say.

"Why a dachshund?"

"When we lived in Abidjan on the Ivory Coast my parents got a dachshund puppy and called it Villette."

"After the Brontë novel?"

"How many chemical engineers read Charlotte Brontë?"

"Quite a few Indian ones. A few Brits. No Americans. Go on with your story," Bhima says.

"Well, remember I told you I was sent to boarding school in England when I was ten?"

"As I said before, barbaric."

"Not to the British."

"There's a lot that isn't considered barbaric to the British," Bhima says.

"True. Anyway, I was sent to boarding school in England because Mum and Dad were moving from Kenya to West Africa for Dad's work. My brother and I would fly out to see our parents for the school holidays. They lived in a townhouse with a mango tree and an avocado tree in the garden, a cat, and a tan miniature dachshund called Villette, who I loved and carried about with me everywhere."

"Cute."

"Every morning she would fly down the stairs when I called her and land in the center of a large orange beanbag. I would scoop her up in my arms, carry her with me wherever I could, and at night she'd sleep with her back pressed against mine.

"Leaving her at the end of the holidays was agony for both of us. I was an imaginative child and remember saying goodbye to Villette when the long summer holidays were over and saying to myself, 'Little did she know she would never see her little dog again.'"

"Like someone in a Brontë novel," Bhima says, laughing.

"Yes. But the sad thing is, I was right. I somehow knew I wouldn't see her again. And I didn't. A few weeks later, a man jumped over the wall and took her away."

"Oh, no," Bhima says.

"I always assumed she'd been sold to another family and perhaps loved by another girl who did not know that she used to love me. But my brothers told me recently she was probably eaten. I've wanted a dachshund ever since. But I keep finding other rescues."

"Some of them human."

"Perhaps . . ."

❊ ❊ ❊

"Are you afraid of death?" I ask Bhima again one evening as we sit at either end of his couch, the soles of our bare feet pressed together in the middle.

"Not at all," he says again.

"What do you think happens after death?"

"Nothing," Bhima says.

As usual, he's lying with his head resting on his hands behind his head.

"We're atoms, Alison. We just go back into the Earth. You know I'm an atheist."

"No you're not."

I can see his white teeth in the moonlight. He's laughing.

"Yes, Alison, I am."

"You can't be. You're a scientist, therefore you know there is always the possibility that you might be wrong. Besides, I've seen the peace that falls on you when you're in the woods. I've seen you connect with what you call nature and what some people call God. It's just semantics."

"You think so, do you?"

"I do indeed."

"Come here."

Then, later, in the dark of the night with the candle flickering near one of the windows and the trees being blown by a fierce wind outside, Bhima says, "Why aren't you writing, Alison?"

"Because I'm happy."

"Come on, Alison," he says. "You should be writing."

"I can only bear to write when I have to, Bhima. And right now I just want to be happy."

Still later, in the middle of the night, Bhima half wakes, reaches for me, and after we've made love again, whispers in my ear, "Let's find you a dachshund. You'll have nothing to fear. If anyone tries to take him away from you, they'll have me to contend with."

CHAPTER 30

Then it's March 2020. And the pandemic hits.
Despite the early spin, Bhima knows the world is in serious trouble.

Tom has been staying in Savannah, Georgia during the pandemic. I'm worried about him so I tell Bhima I am driving down to see him.

"Don't go yet," Bhima says. "The virus is rampant. Wait two or three months. Please."

So I do.

My workday hasn't changed all that much because I'm used to working in isolation anyway, but the fear the world is experiencing also penetrates the little towns of Stockbridge and Bennington. We hear ambulances throughout the day, and we hear of friends dying.

Bhima only meets with his staff outside in the parking lot and they all wear masks. Apart from them, the only person he sees is me.

Bhima really needs a haircut and somewhat nervously hands me some scissors. I don't know how, but the haircut I give him is, if I say it myself, rather splendid.

"You look like a French movie star," I say.

"Merci," Bhima says.

When we are together everything is okay. Until Bhima turns on his iPhone and reads the news. Then he becomes tense and angry and paces his house, increasingly appalled and outraged by it all.

When I am with him, I do everything I can to stop him focusing on the news and I succeed. But only when I am with him.

Bhima's cardiologist tells him it is vital he does not expose himself to COVID because of his triple bypass and that if he gets COVID he will most likely die.

I am extra careful, seeing no one, so I can be with Bhima as often as possible without putting him at risk.

I'm also still worried about Tom, who is on his own at nineteen, and so in June I drive through the pandemic to spend three weeks in Savannah with Tom, Lucy, and a friend of Lucy's, who fly in a few days after I arrive. Bhima isn't at all happy about my driving down alone.

"It's an eighteen-hour drive!" he says.

"I like driving!" I say. "It'll be fun."

During the three weeks we are apart, I call Bhima every night and find him in a state of high anxiety.

"Have you seen the statistics? COVID is a mess. The disinformation is dangerous at best. I can't seem to rest," Bhima says.

"Take a break from the news, go on a walk, go outside. Turn off the news for a while. Please, Bhima."

But he's not listening to me.

"I called my cardiologist because I wanted to play tennis harder and my heart wouldn't let me and he wouldn't see me in person because of COVID so he halved my beta blocker medication over the phone. When are you coming home?"

"I'm feeling so irritable," Bhima says not long after I return. "My heart's been beating too fast again. I'm wondering if halving the medication was a mistake."

"Call your cardiologist," I say.

Bhima calls his cardiologist, who repeats that he's not seeing people in person because of COVID. He tells Bhima that there's always an adjustment period with medication, so Bhima has nothing to worry about.

Mysteriously, a record of that conversation never made it into Bhima's medical report.

We've been apart for three weeks. And we both know we never want to be separated for that long again.

CHAPTER 31

Wednesday, July 22, 2020

I wake up suddenly in the middle of the night. I've screamed again.

"Bad dream?" Bhima says sitting up with me.

"Not really," I say. "An odd one though."

"What was it?"

"I dreamed your elliptical was at my house instead of on your porch. My feet were moving up and down, up and down as I looked out over Stockbridge. You weren't there."

Thursday, July 23, 2020

I ask Bhima all about his triple bypass. He talks for two hours, telling me how he remembered his family standing around his bed, crying. I listen closely to all the details. He tells me where they cut him and how close he came to dying and how hard his recovery was. It took him more than a year.

That night I wake up screaming again.

"Bad dream?"

"Must have been."

"What happened?"

"I don't remember."

"I had a bad dream too," Bhima says.

"What was it?"

"I'm running, looking for someone I've lost. Trying to find them. Longing for them. Trying to reach them. It was terrible. I think the person I was trying to reach is you."

"Come here, Bhima."

Sunday, July 26, 2020

Bhima is stressed and I know he needs a break.

We head to Gedney Farm, a beautiful retreat in New Marlborough in the Berkshires.

There are fields on either side of the drive leading to the property. On one of them is a croquet pitch.

"Do you play croquet?" I ask, pronouncing it "cro-kay."

"More like crick-et," Bhima says, pronouncing it "cri-kay."

Both of us succumb to helpless laughter.

We are the only people staying at Gedney Farm. We go on a walk and we swim for an hour, with Bhima lying on his back in his orange flotation vest and me swimming back and forth, towards him and away from him. The water is soft and silky and the sky a perfect blue.

There's a big jacuzzi bath in our hotel bathroom, which we share with great glee. We enjoy every minute of our first dinner in a restaurant since the pandemic began—we're outside, the waiter is in a mask, there's no one else there.

There is a glow about Bhima that weekend.

The next morning we go on a walk by a river and start talking about what is most important to us, apart from each other.

Bhima says that from now on, he wants to spend more time with old friends he's drifted away from and his family.

"Let's spend some of each year in India," I say.

"Okay," Bhima says.

I tell Bhima that from now on, I want to spend more time with my brothers who I miss terribly, and my family and dear friends in England.

"Let's spend some of each year in England," Bhima says.

"Okay," I say.

Then he says he regrets not seriously answering my father's apology about what the British did to India, and looks forward to many hours talking honestly with him about it next time they see each other.

"I love your parents," Bhima says again.

"They love you," I say.

I tell him that from now on I want to get to know my children even better—now that they're adults. I want to listen to them, fully present. I don't want to waste a minute.

At the heart of our lives we will have each other.

We will create a home together that people we love will come to whenever they wish; we will spend time with the people we love. We will connect more, not less.

"Shall we marry, Alison?" Bhima says.

"Yes," I say.

He is beaming. So am I.

"Everyone will be so happy. Especially my mother. But before we tell anybody, first I must ask your father's permission," Bhima says.

"He'll love that!"

"Will you come and live with me in Vermont when Lucy goes to college in September?"

"I will, but . . ."

"But?"

"If I'm coming to Bennington, I would like to paint the walls of your house a lighter color and find some cheerful rugs to brighten up the place."

Bhima is grinning.

"No problem. We will Alisonify the house."

"I'd also like to bring my keyboard, because I want to start playing the piano better!" I say.

"I will buy you a baby grand."

"My keyboard will be fine, Bhima."

"No," Bhima says. "I will buy you a baby grand. You play so beautifully!"

I really don't. Bhima just thinks I do.

The only time he has heard me play was at his brother's house in New Jersey when the family gathered to celebrate his brother's fiftieth birthday. I felt utterly at home in the heart of Bhima's family.

I sat down at the piano and started improvising something tender that reflected how I felt about them all. About Bhima. About us.

"I heard you," Bhima says from across the room. "I was standing at the door, listening."

"Yes."

I smile at him then return to my laptop.

On July 26, Bhima and I decide to spend the rest of our lives together. I'll bring my recording studio to Bhima's basement so I can narrate audiobooks there, and I'll play him made-up tunes in the evenings while he finishes his work. We'll be together every night. At ease. At peace. Together. For the rest of our lives.

❄ ❄ ❄

Usually, I go to Bhima's house on Fridays, but on Friday, July 29, 2020, I can't because I'm giving a speech to a group of adoptees via Zoom. Which is something I haven't done in years.

When *The English American* came out, I went around the country doing fundraising benefits for adoption and foster care organizations. I'd try to get people to understand why the laws prohibiting adopted people from having access to their original birth certificates did so much more harm than good.

I'd tell jokes and talk about why someone from a very happy adoptive family might need to find out more about the people she came from. I'd try to help adoptive parents understand how in need of encouragement even the most apparently confident adopted kids always are.

Now, I want to encourage my fellow adoptees to dare to fall in love.

I tell them I understand how terrifying it can be for someone who has been abandoned to trust in love, but after fifty years I've finally taken the leap and I have never—ever—been so happy.

I tell them you don't need to have a relationship with a dog or a human that you don't realllllly want because you think you won't ever get what you want.

"I know some of the adoption experts love to say adopted people are doomed because we experienced this thing when we were babies so we'll never be able to trust anyone enough to truly love. But if I can do it, you can. I know it's scary. But I promise you, if you take this step, you'll get to travel through life without having to experience its gnawing, abject loneliness. And the dif ference is unimaginable."

It's too late to drive to Bhima's that night. So I go in the morning.

CHAPTER 32

Saturday, July 30, 2020

I drive to see Bhima in Bennington.

It's a soft summer's day. We think we might spend Saturday riding electric bikes, but Bhima says he's feeling tired.

So we lie down for awhile, then we play rummy.

Then Bhima says, "Alison, let's go outside and look at the stars."

Bhima has a large telescope that his family gave him for his fiftieth birthday that he has never used, and that night he insists on carrying it himself through the woods. It's a hot and humid night. Bhima is wearing a cloth tartan shirt and a pair of shorts with no socks. I follow behind Bhima, carrying a blanket, which I put on the ground when we get through the trees to the top of the hill.

I sit on the blanket and watch Bhima concentrating intently as he looks through the telescope at the stars.

"We are all made from the stars, Alison. Every living thing comes from stardust," he says.

We get home, we play some more rummy, then we go to bed.

❈ ❈ ❈

Sunday, July 31, 2020

By 9:00 a.m. Bhima is downstairs watching the car racing. I watch him from the railing above.

"Are you okay?" I ask him.

"I'm feeling a bit tired actually," he says.

"Let's rest," I say.

Bhima has never slept in the daytime since I've known him. But he agrees to lie down on the bed. I'm not tired, so I start to get up.

"Don't leave me," he says.

That too is a first.

"I won't," I say.

I lie back down, put some headphones on and watch something on my computer while he sleeps next to me.

Three hours later when he wakes up, I give him some ginger, carrot, and apple juice.

I feel his forehead. He has a fever. He says he has indigestion. I find some Tums.

We call the doctor, who tells us to get Bhima a COVID test ASAP.

For the first time ever Bhima hands me the car keys and asks me to drive.

"Maybe you'll have a tiny bit of COVID and it will act as a kind of vaccine, so it'll turn out to be a good thing," I say as I drive as fast as I can down the driveway and towards Bennington.

Bhima smiles. "Oh, Alison, you can find the positive in absolutely anything."

At the hospital there's a security guard in a mask who says they're not testing for COVID in the ER, so we have to walk over to the pulmonary center.

Bhima looks exhausted but the guard won't let me go in with him because of COVID. I say, "Please. He's had a triple bypass. He needs me . . ."

"No," she says.

"Then make sure you don't leave him alone. He's had a triple bypass . . ." And then I watch Bhima walk slowly into the building.

❋   ❋   ❋

3:00 p.m., Alison Larkin: You okay?

One minute later Bhima sends me the only picture of himself he ever took. He's in a hospital chair wearing a mask, breathing through an inhaler.

3:05 p.m., Bhima Nitta: They've given me this inhaler. Supposed to help me breathe, apparently. And they're testing me for COVID.

3:06 p.m., Alison Larkin: I love you.

✳ ✳ ✳

Half an hour later the security guard comes over and tells me they left Bhima alone in the room and when they came back they found him on the floor in cardiac arrest. They tried to get a heartbeat but couldn't for twenty minutes. Then they got a heartbeat. Now they've put him in an induced coma and they're flying him in a helicopter to the Albany Medical Center.

They won't let me fly in the helicopter with him because of COVID, so I drive the hour to get there.

The doctor tells me that because the Albany Medical Center is in New York and he collapsed in Vermont, they don't have access to his medical records.

"It would help us to know what medications he is taking," someone says.

So I drive an hour back to Bennington and call the hospital and read the medications over the phone. There are a lot of them.

Over the next two days while Bhima's in his coma with tubes sticking out of him, I talk to him. And I sing to him. And when they make me leave because visitors are only allowed four hours at a time because of COVID, I leave my audiobook of *Great Expectations* playing next to him so he can hear my voice.

Everything's going to be alright, I tell myself. He'll wake up from his coma, like people do in the movies, and say, "Hallo, beautiful woman."

But I'm on my way to the hospital the next day when his brother calls and tells me they've done a brain scan. Bhima isn't there anymore.

Four hours later this brilliant, beautiful, exceptional fifty-four-year-old man is pronounced dead.

If we are made from stardust,
A star is what we are

Perhaps you have gone back up there
If you have it's awfully far.
What happened? Where are you, baby?

CHAPTER 33

Bhima's sister said, "He should have died in the motorcycle accident, but he did not. He should have died in the car crash, but he did not. He definitely should have died during the triple bypass, but he did not. We are all convinced that he stayed around to know true happiness with you."

On the surface of things I'm functioning calmly and well. In fact, I am completely numb and it is the numbness that allows me to get through the funeral, which for everyone but Bhima's immediate family and me has to happen on Zoom.

Bhima's family flies through the pandemic from California and Florida to Bennington, where I am waiting for them. I hold Bhima's mother in my arms when she gets out of the car. She feels frail and yet there's a strength coming from her too.

"She's stronnnnng, Alison. Like you."

Suddenly, Bhima's two brothers and sister and their spouses are in Bhima's house. In our house. In the house we were going to live in together. In the house where we ate together and slept together and fell in love.

They're talking and reminiscing and crying and laughing and I watch them through a haze and serve them the Indian food that I asked my friend Tony to pick up from a nearby restaurant. I'm still numb.

And with Bhima's entire family around me, I sleep in our bed under the golden comforter we slept under together just a few nights before.

The funeral is delayed because of course Bhima was an organ donor, so two kidneys, one liver, and two corneas went to people who needed them. The ultimate recycling.

Bhima's mother tells me to take any of the clothes I want, so I take his jacket and socks and our comforter and his washing bag with his silver tongue scraper and Listerine and razor and deodorant and put them in a bag in the back of my car and drive home to be with Lucy.

There are ten people at the funeral home in North Bennington, all socially distanced, all wearing masks. Bhima's body lies in an open casket, dressed in the suit he wore at the Lit Net Gala. His lips are sewn together. He looks shiny, as if he has been waxed. As if he is just sleeping.

His brother has set up a camera so the funeral can be watched by Bhima's Indian family and friends all the over world, including Mum and Dad, who have never used Zoom before.

Bhima's brother is halfway through his eulogy when everybody watching hears my Dad's very English voice speaking very loudly to Mum.

"Is that Bhima's brother?" Dad says. "It looks like he's standing on his head!"

"I think you've got the iPad upside down, Rob. Turn the iPad the other way up," Mum says.

And from all over the world, Bhima's always-polite Indian family and my friends are sending messages to my parents saying, "Could you please press the mute button?"

"What's a mute button?" Dad shouts.

"I think it's the little button on the bottom left of the screen," Mum says, shouting back, so Dad can hear.

"Now Alison's standing on her head," Dad roars. "What is going on?"

Bhima would have loved it.

Later I watch my body from above as we all watch Bhima's body being put in a big steel oven where he is cremated. And somehow I manage to drive home.

"There were elements of my funeral that were pure Monty Python," Bhima says, here, today, from the couch.

"Yes."

The laughter starts small and builds until we're laughing helplessly, here, today, in the quiet of my little house in Stockbridge, two years after he died.

CHAPTER 34

"Bravo!" Bhima is clapping.

"But I haven't got to the end yet!"

"I know. But it's time to take a break."

I've been staring at the screen for hours. I stand up, stretch and suddenly realize I'm hungry.

Bhima has made some dal and rice and is eating it with a piece of naan. He can eat whatever he wants these days. He's taller than before—stronger, much.

"You need to eat something, Alison. Then you need to rest. Then you need to write down everything that's happened since I kicked the bucket."

Bhima's eyes are alight with mischief.

"Sanity is overrated, Alison," Bhima says, reading my mind. "Let's rest now. You can go back to writing the story of what happened next first thing in the morning."

"You're as relentless as Archbishop Desmond Tutu," I say, lying down next to him, already drifting off to sleep.

"Hey, what's the worst that can happen?" he whispers.

"Very funny, Bhima."

CHAPTER 35

I've come to the conclusion that it is actually quite useful to have had early trauma or loss of some kind. So when the worst happens again there's a part of you that goes, "Ah yes! I remember this!" Sort of like a muscle you haven't used in a long time but is familiar when you start using it again.

I like to think of it as a kind of perk.

No one comes into my house, because it's the pandemic, but everyone in my little town knows what has happened because it has been in the papers. Neighbors in masks keep appearing at my back door with food. I don't have the heart to tell them I can't eat anything, so I thank them profusely through the window, but after dark, I take the food over to one of the Bobs, saying I've already eaten lots and it'll go bad if someone doesn't eat it.

I lose twelve pounds in the first two weeks. It's not a diet I'd recommend, but it works.

August 15, 2020

Today I make myself get dressed.

I wear the orange linen dress Bhima loved and a pair of white sandals. I manage to find a hairbrush, which is always a challenge, and pull it through my hair, which looked like a nest when I woke up this morning.

I'm sleeping okay, thanks to Alka-Seltzer PM. The doctor suggested lorazepam if the adrenaline shots come too quickly, but I don't want to take drugs. So I'm not going to.

My body is moving normally. Apparently I still know how to drive, so that's good.

When I get to the post office I remember I have to wear

my mask. Where the hell is it? Damn! I left it at home. No, wait. There's one on the floor of the car underneath a sock. What's that doing there?

I put on the mask, head into the little post office, scrabble about in my handbag for my post office box key, and I'm just about to open my box when I feel a hand on my shoulder. I look and see an older, weather-beaten hand belonging to a masked American woman of about sixty-five or seventy with steel-gray hair.

Who is this person? She's staring at me as if she knows me.

Oh! Right! It's Mabel. She used to be a primary school teacher, now she gardens and looks after dogs.

Her eyes are watery over her paper mask.

"It's going to take a long long long long long long long long long long long long time," she says.

I nod and half smile at her. She can't see my expression because I'm wearing my mask, which is probably a good thing. I say, "Thank you," and try to turn away, but she hasn't finished.

I turn politely back.

"And you need to know there are a lot more than just five stages of grief," Mabel says.

"Oh, yes?" I say.

"After shock and denial, there'll be pain and guilt, sadness, anger, desperation, bargaining with God ('I'll become a nicer person if you can just bring him back' kinda thing), loneliness, frustration, depression, despair, and suicidal thoughts. It's going to be really really really really really really really really hard."

She looks triumphant.

I thank her and turn toward my mail.

One of the things I like most about my post office is that there are two big bins in which you can throw away unwanted mail so it doesn't clutter up your house. I flick through today's pile in the vain hope that there might be something from the hospital telling me how Bhima died, throw away the junk mail trying to sell me insurance and—dear GOD—retirement funds already?

Then I drive home as quickly as I can so I can lie on my own in the dark, thinking about Bhima.

Of course I'm not alone. An old friend who I haven't seen

for years calls me from England.

"It was the same for me when Johnny died," she says

"I'm so sorry. Johnny? How long were you together?"

"Fourteen years. He was my soulmate. I buried him where he was happiest. In the garden. He used to love running around in circles burying his bones."

August 26, 2020

The phone rings.

"How are you?" Mum asks.

"I'll be fine, Mum," I say. "You?"

"Honestly? We're completely fed up with this silly COVIS!"

I'd correct her, but it brings me almost as much joy as my daughter's mispronunciation of "sun scream" until she was about nine.

"It's all very boring, darling," Mum says. "We can't play bridge or see any of our friends. And they've canceled Scottish dancing."

August 27, 2020

I've been receiving emails and calls from Bhima's family and friends and people I didn't even know existed. Like this one.

From: John Branson

Time: 11:17 a.m.

I heard about Bhima, the "Power Guru," not long after returning to Shaftsbury, Vermont 5 years ago. I finally got to meet him on the bus on our way back from a Chamber of Commerce trip. I always said a glad hello whenever I saw him in public, which was mostly at Arts Exchange events. That's where I met you. What a nice couple, I said to my companion. Look how happy they are.

What a shame that his and your life together was cut short. I believe we get that metaphor straight from the Fates. I feel for you. It's as if Ganesh passed through this town in the person of Bhima. What right did we have to hold on to a god?

August 28, 2020

Bhima's ex-girlfriend, Nicole, arrives at my home in Stock-bridge. Somehow she has managed to get Bhima's incredibly heavy elliptical machine onto her red pickup truck and drive it all the way here from Bennington.

As soon as I see the thing I remember the last time I used it. On Bhima's porch. Less than three weeks ago. When he was very much alive.

I was watching something on my laptop while I worked out, and he was doing an online strength class inside.

We drank water. We ate dinner. We made love. We went to bed.

Today, Nicole and I manage to get the elliptical off the truck by dragging it onto my porch on one of the orange cushions my friend Sasha gave me that go with her old garden furniture.

I decide to write to Bhima as if he were there.

August 29, 2020

Dear Bhima,

I went to church and Mary Boyce asked me how I was and I told her I don't know why you died.

Mary told me to go home to England but there's a two-week quarantine for anyone going to England and I don't want to kill my parents by giving them COVID.

She said she thought your anxiety was a sign—that the beta blockers being halved must have had some-thing to do with it. That something was going on with your heart.

Would you still be alive if your cardiologist had seen you in person when you told him you felt "off?"

At 4:02 p.m. today I felt something kick my heart and I started to panic. I somehow knew that was the time you died. Two weeks ago to the second. On the Sun-day I took you in for a COVID test. A COVID TEST!

Did you send me the photo because you were trying to tell me something? Did they kill you in there?

I somehow managed today to record the last two chapters of the audiobook I was narrating when I last saw you. When I told Erick at Dreamscape why the book will be a day late, I've never delivered anything late, he said, "Alison, it's only an audiobook. Take your time."

August 30, 2020

There's a nip in the air. Fall is coming.

Today the numbness thawed for a minute or so. I was sitting outside the coffee shop with the Bobs admiring a new drawing by Bob's daughter, the artist Phoebe Helanger, when I felt tears rolling down my cheeks. Damn.

I thought I'd covered it well enough, that's what shirt sleeves and an acting training are for after all, but an hour after I leave the coffee shop, Alan shows up at my house on his bicycle "just to say hi."

Then Bob shows up on his bike "just to say hi."

Then another Bob "just happens" to be passing by in his pick up truck. This Bob is seventy-five but strong and fit and he jumps out of his truck in his muddy boots and plaid shirt. "I brought you a fire pit, Alison," he says gruffly.

Then, without asking, he takes a fire pit and a propane tank out of the back of his truck, lifts them onto my back porch, hooks the whole thing up and moves my outdoor furniture around it.

Then he shows me how to turn the propane tank on and off. "Don't forget, "Righty Tighty, Lefty Loosey."

Then he says, "This way you can have people over without getting COVID."

"Are you sure?" I say, delighted.

"You're doin' me a favor. This old thing was just taking up space in my garage."

Sure, Bob. The propane tank is brand new.

CHAPTER 36

Aug 31, 2020

Dear Bhima,

I make it to the post office this morning without having to interact with anyone and I'm almost in my car when there's a shout from the direction of the coffee shop.

"Alison! Hey! Alison!"

I look up. Perhaps it's one of the Bobs? No, they're never here at this time of day.

It's Chris, the sixty-year-old father of one of my son's friends, who appears to be thundering across the road in my direction.

"Something HORRIBLE happened to you, didn't it?" Chris says, slightly out of breath, when he gets to me.

"Did something really HORRIBLE happen to you?"

"Well, my fiancé died," I mutter.

"That's right! He died suddenly, right outta the blue! I read about it in the paper. Let me buy you a coffee."

"Tea please," I say.

"Iced?"

"No, thank you."

"You Brits," Chris says, laughing.

I sit outside the coffee shop with my face to the sun, hiding behind my sunglasses.

Chris brings me a cup of tea. Then he begins talking.

He starts by telling me why COVID is a hoax.

Then he tells me why being made to wear a mask is a violation of his rights.

Then he tells me that he has read everything there is to read about vaccines, and that they're an attempt by Bill Gates to take over the human race and that they cause heart attacks, but I'm not really listening.

Instead, I'm enjoying sipping my very hot tea on this very hot day, which is what people like to do in India. Chris's mouth is still moving and I'm thinking of you. Wondering where you are. Wondering if you died of COVID. Wondering what you would say if you were here.

Chris is an intelligent man in so many ways. And yet he truly believes what he is saying. Yet another American with absolutely no understanding of science.

You were as polite as I am. Usually. Except when people were being hypocritical.

Like the woman, Margaret Something-or-Other, who said she was so concerned about climate change she might consider buying a hybrid car but she'd never get a fully electric car because she didn't want to be stranded on the highway.

I was sitting next to you when she said this. We were at the only dinner party we ever went to with friends, because we preferred to spend our precious time alone together. But I made you go because Tony Eprile and Judy Schwartz are old friends of mine and we'd turned down their invitations so many times and I loved them too much to turn down another.

Judy wrote *Cows Save the Planet*, which I knew you'd find interesting, and Tony's father was actively involved in the Anti-Apartheid movement and knew Nelson Mandela.

He is also one of the best cooks I know.

You seemed to be having a reasonably good time talking to Margaret. Until she made the comment about the car.

I was sitting next to you and instantly felt the tension fill your entire being.

"You are a highly intelligent woman," you said to

Margaret. Everyone at the table had stopped talking and people were listening carefully. And politely. To you.

My ear was attuned to your Indian accent but I was aware on this occasion and a few others that people had to listen carefully to understand you sometimes.

I loved that you refused to Americanize your Indian accent even though you certainly could have.

"You understand how catastrophic the situation is regarding climate change," you said, turning to Margaret. "And you are relatively affluent, yes?"

"Yes," Margaret said.

"So, if someone like you who can easily afford an electric vehicle won't get one because it might cause you mild inconvenience, then actually you are worse than the people who don't understand how serious the situation is. You are certainly a big part of the problem."

Everyone paused for a nanosecond. Then you started eating again and so did everyone else. I saw Judy look at Tony and then at you and then at me.

I remember putting my hand on your arm and taking a breath, hoping you would do the same.

You did.

How I loved you in that moment.

A week after you died, Margaret emailed me a long, kind message.

"Seeing the love between you and Bhima was an honor, Alison. It was a special kind of love that I feel privileged to have witnessed."

People who met us when we were together are all saying the same sort of thing.

Chris is still talking and I am still nodding and giving every appearance of listening. But I don't hear a word. My mind is still on a loop.

Was it stress over what was happening in the world that killed you, Bhima?

Was it COVID?

The morning of the day you died, after we realized you

had a fever and were heading into Bennington for a COVID test, you started pacing.

"I bet Neil gave me COVID!" you said.

"The guy you had lunch with this week? The one with the little plane?"

"Yes!"

You were going to take flying lessons and then fly with me above the world, just the two of us, for years and years and years.

"Yes! Neil got waaaaaay too close to me. And he wasn't wearing a mask!" you said before we left your house, about two hours before you died.

The doctors said the COVID test was negative, but how did they know? What if they tested too early? If it wasn't COVID, why was there fluid in your lungs?

"Pneumonia?" they wondered.

Huh?

They were so quick to be done with you. The hospital doctor in the mask telling me it was over, that your brilliant brain was dead. But that your organs were strong and would be useful, so they'd keep you alive long enough to "harvest" them.

"Why did he go into cardiac arrest?" I asked the doctor.

"We don't know."

"Is there some sort of report I could see?"

"The folks at the Southern Vermont Medical Center will have to send it to you. He was in an induced coma by the time he got to us."

It's not my place to ask any more questions. We weren't married yet, and the questions must be asked by your family.

Even they can't get the records until your brother gets power of attorney. COVID is slowing down the already slow administrative processes even more.

Was it my fault? Did the chocolate and avocado pudding I made you the night before you died have too much caffeine in it and set your heart beating too fast or something?

Was it COVID?

No one at the hospital seems to know or care why you died so suddenly. Why not? Is it because you were Indian?

Chris's mouth is still moving.

Now Chris is saying that everyone's overreacted to COVID so people are dying because they can't get in to see their doctors.

Is that why you died? Because the cardiologist you revered (who probably got his degree online) wouldn't see you in person because he was afraid of getting COVID?

Oh good. Chris has finally stopped talking. This means I can thank him for the tea and head home. To lie in the dark thinking of you.

CHAPTER 37

September 1, 2020

My hairdresser, Mark, at the Seven Salon Spa is married to the African American artist Pops Peterson, who recently had an exhibition at the Norman Rockwell Museum. Hair salon admin half the time, nationally renowned artist the rest of the time. Only in the Berkshires.

When they heard what had happened, Mark and Pops gave me a gift certificate for a massage with Alex, who is Russian and very funny.

I'm acutely aware that the last person to touch me was you.

I tell Alex you died three weeks ago.

"Don't think of anything sad," Alex says, and we both laugh. "Of course you are at high risk, coming to me. Being Russian I have four legs and no arms. We are all corrupt, as you know. It is very dangerous to be massaged by a Russian."

"Just don't put a microchip in my neck."

"I might, I might not."

My body is tense and everything hurts, and for an hour Alex and I are cracking jokes and the laughter eases things.

When I stand up, I feel dizzy and sit back down again.

Alex waits with me for the next twenty minutes, continuing our banter until my legs have stopped wobbling and it is safe for me to go home.

September 2, 2020

Today someone gave me a gift certificate for a facial with Maria.

I'm lying down, breathing in steam, wearing a mask that

smells of avocado.

"I had only just met my husband—like, I had only known him a month, that was all, when his son died," Maria says. Her manner is gentle and kind. The hugging that usually takes place when people die isn't allowed because of COVID. I had to test twice before being allowed in the facial room.

"My husband said then and still says that he's sure he met me so he would not be alone when he went through the loss of his son. There's always a reason. You were there so Bhima would not have to die alone."

That's her theory.

Your sister said, "It was Bhima's time to die, Alison. No matter where he was or what he was doing, this was his time to die. There was nothing anyone could do about it." That's a Hindu belief, I gather.

Where are you?

September 3, 2020

Tom usually only calls when he needs money.

"Hey, Mom."

"Hi, Tom."

"Hi."

"Is your rent due?"

"No. I just—you know. I wanted to check on you."

"That's nice," I say. "I'm glad you're okay."

"You okay, Mom?"

"I will be, darling. I promise."

Damn. I'm crying again.

Lucy was cast as one of the ugly sisters in *Cinderella* when the pandemic hit and she, like every other teenager in the world, was yanked away from her peers and into isolation.

Despite all that, my brilliant daughter has managed to get a scholarship to college, which is a huge help because despite Tom also landing a scholarship, he's at film school so it's still costing every penny we have.

Don't get me started on the cost of American college. Just don't.

Lucy has been staying with her dad in his family cabin in Maine where he's working remotely because of the pandemic. But I know Lucy needs to come home and I need to be here—fully—when she gets here.

I must come back from this.

September 4, 2020

Dear Bhima,

Do you remember the psychic woman who rented my studio for her podcast? Vicki Cowley? The one whose husband died? She asked about you when we went on a walk today and I told her the details of your last days. "I wish I knew why he died," I said in conclusion. "Maybe it was my fault."

"Why do you say that?"

"Well, he had indigestion. Maybe it was my cooking?"

We were walking through the woods in Lenox.

"He was having a heart attack all week, that's what I'm getting." Vicki said.

She's a nice woman, and hearing this made me feel a little better, but there is no way she can possibly know. Then she asked to see a recent photo of you, so I showed her the pic of the two of us by the river moments after we decided to spend the rest of our lives together.

You were wearing your orange checked shirt, and I was in the white dress you loved.

"You see the crinkle at the side of Bhima's eyes, Alison?" Vicki said.

"Yes."

"You can tell from that that when this photo was taken he didn't have long. How long was this taken before he died?"

"Less than a week."

"He was getting ready to leave. It's all there in his eyes."

Oh, for God's sake. But . . .

September 5, 2020

Dear Bhima,

I would love to know who inherited your corneas.
Does this person see because of you?
I would love to know who inherited your liver and
your kidneys. Do those people live because of you?
You brother says it could be months before we see the
hospital reports.
What happened?

CHAPTER 38

September 6, 2020

Exactly one month since you were declared dead, I'm in an acupuncture room in Great Barrington and the guy leaves me alone in the room.

I'm lying on my stomach with needles in my back, unable to move.

Then, I sense someone sitting in the corner of the acupuncture room, in the dark. Relaxed and present.

No way.

"Bhima? Is that you?"

"You're paying this guy a hundred dollars to stick needles in your back? Are you out of your mind?" you say. I know it's my imagination. But I start to laugh anyway.

That is exactly what you would say. Exactly.

And then I'm having trouble breathing. Damn this mask. I take it off and shut my eyes, and I'm no longer me, alone, in the acupuncture room.

Instead I'm you. Bhima. Alone. In the room in the Southern Vermont Medical Center. Just after you got my last text.

"I love you," I texted.

You have just seen my text. You've put the phone down.

You're wearing a mask.

You can't breathe.

You're clutching at your heart.

You're falling to the floor.

You're choking on something. Vomit maybe?

You try to call out, but you can't make a loud enough sound because you can't breathe.

No one is coming.

You're frightened.

Then you're gone.

Now I'm back, lying alone on my tummy on the acupuncture table.

I'm frightened.

"Hallo?" I call out.

The acupuncturist is treating someone else in another room.

I call out again.

"Help!"

The acupuncturist comes into the room in a hurry.

"Could you please take the, uh, the needles out of my back?" I say.

"Yes," he says.

I tell him what happened.

"So you saw your fiancé?" he says.

"Not really. I mean, I imagined him . . ."

"They come during treatments. Quite a lot, actually."

Oh, come *on*. What is this? *The Sixth Sense?*

He's trying to make me feel better. Nice man. I can't get out of there fast enough.

I know it's my imagination. I'm not psychotic.

But there's a part of me that's sure I've just relived Bhima's last moments. And something has been released.

They left him alone.

He clutched at his heart.

He was choking.

He couldn't breathe.

He fell to the floor.

They did not come.

And it was over.

CHAPTER 39

September 14, 2020

My heart aches. I'm deeply tired. There's division and bigotry and hate on all sides. The news is full of despair.

I can't bear any of it.

I am driving along Route 7 before dawn.

"You're driving too fast!" I almost hear you say.

"Ha! You can talk! You were a certified racing car driver for years."

"Yes, but I drove too fast on the racetrack at Lime Rock, not on Route 7!"

"After you died, your brother told me that when he was a teenager you took him for a spin and drove the car at over 120 miles per hour. What was that about?"

"I was a risk-taker."

"Too damn right."

I put my foot on the accelerator.

"I'm a risk taker too. But the risks I take are usually in my work."

Like spending months and months writing a book with no idea if anyone will ever read it or if it will get published.

Like performing a one-woman show in front of thousands of people.

Like leaving the life you know when you're a young woman to meet the woman who gave you birth, who, instead of solving your problems, creates more.

Like taking the risk of falling fully in love for the first time at the age of fifty-five and . . .

"Damn!"

"Slow down, beautiful woman," you say again.

Tears are streaming down my face.

I'm in the car and no one can hear me.

"Bhimmmaaaaaaaaa!"

"SLOW DOWN BEAUTIFUL WOMAN!"

No one ever called me beautiful before. Pretty? Sometimes. Attractive? Yes. But never beautiful. Dear GOD, the world's going to hell. What's the point!

"Slow down, Alison."

I press my foot down harder on the accelerator.

"Bhimaaaaaaaaaaa!"

And then there's a siren blaring and lights flashing and I have no choice but to slow down and pull over to the side of the road.

The cop parks in front of me, just by Lovers Lane, and gets out of his car with his gun hanging obviously from his belt holster.

"License and registration, ma'am."

Where the hell are they? Of course—they're under the hairbrush and the chocolate Yasso yoghurt wrapper in the glove compartment. I hand them to him. They're a little sticky.

"Do you know how fast you were going, ma'am?" the young man says.

"Seventy, maybe?" I say. "I'm not sure. I was looking at the road, not the speedometer."

"Ninety-five," the cop says.

Oh, dear.

A car drives past, lighting up the policeman's face so I can see it clearly for the first time.

"Mark?" I say.

He looks up. "Ms. Larkin?!"

"It's Alison . . . You're a policeman now?"

"Sure am," Mark says.

I can see the pride in his face, and it's well-deserved.

"A cop! Now that's something I'd never have predicted, not in a million years," I say, laughing uproariously.

The laughter brings me back into the real world, which hurts so damn much to live in. Except when you're laughing.

I mean, it really is funny. Mark was one of the students who

I taught stand-up comedy to for a semester. Why? Because I figured if the kids like my son were into taking risks—big ones—why not get them hooked on the high of making people laugh before some bastard robbed them of their light and life and talent, got them hooked on heroin or oxytocin and destroyed not only their lives but the lives of everyone who loved them?

Mark was adopted. I'm remembering the day he came into class in tears. He was about seventeen at the time.

"What's up?" I asked him.

"I just found out that my birth father sold drugs in Guatemala. Not only that, he was the head of a drug cartel. Now he's in jail."

"Whoa," I said.

He told me more. I got it. I mean, I really got it, obviously, as I too was an adopted person who'd had to somehow integrate the truth about her biological heritage into her sense of her own identity. But it took years, starting when I was twenty-eight, not when I was seventeen.

"No wonder I'm messed up," I remember Mark saying when he told me.

"You're not messed up," I remember saying. "And I see this as quite promising news, actually."

"Why?"

"The only thing you inherit from your birth parents is your DNA. Your sense of right and wrong comes from your environment and from you."

"Yeah. So . . . ?"

"Well, if your birth father sold drugs and was the head of a drug cartel, you know he was a good salesman and he was a leader. If he'd chosen to sell ideas and gone into politics, for example, well maybe he could have been president of Guatemala by now. All you inherit from him is some of his DNA. But you get to choose to do what you want with it."

I remember holding my breath until I saw the flash of understanding cross his young face.

Now I know he heard me, because instead of heading in the same direction as his birth father, Mark chose to become a cop. A COP! Go figure . . .

"You were *funny*, too!" I say, remembering.

"My stand-up tape helped me get into college," he says.

"And now you're a cop!" I say. "Do you like it?"

"Yeah, I love it!" he says. Then, "Are you okay, Ms. Larkin?"

I know there won't be any tell-tale mascara running down my face, because I don't wear makeup—I can never find it. But I'm conscious of the fact that I've been crying and the kid is intuitive, plus he has what the British call a torch and the Americans insist on calling a flashlight, and he's been shining it in my direction.

"Are you okay, Ms. Larkin?" Mark says again.

I nod.

"I'm going to let you off with a caution this time. But you can't speed like that again."

"I won't."

He bangs the top of my car with his hand and walks off, grinning.

"He could have taken your license for driving that fast and then you'd be well and truly fucked," Bhima says.

"I know."

"You could have killed yourself. Or someone else!"

"I would never drive that fast if there was anyone else on the road."

"Alison!!!!"

Now I'm talking to Bhima out loud. Great.

There's a shift somewhere and I swear I hear Bhima's voice whispering from somewhere deep inside me.

"Alison, wanting to die doesn't mean you don't want to live anymore. It just means you want to live differently."

It was something I said to him once, when he told me about a challenging time in his own life.

"So now you're quoting me to me?" I say.

"I am."

"Bhima?"

I take a deep breath. Silence.

I start to drive.

The sun is coming up, slowly, over the golf course.

The light is golden, orange, red.

CHAPTER 40

September 18, 2020

I haven't spoken to anyone but Mark the policeman in two days.

The phone rings.

"Come to Cape Cod and stay with us for a few days, Ali," my friend Barb says.

"But what about COVID?"

"Forget COVID, just come."

It's a lifeline.

I throw some clothes and a toothbrush into the back of my car and drive to Cape Cod.

By the by, slinging your clothes in the back of the car rather than packing them neatly in a suitcase is genetic. The first time my American birth father came to visit, I was delighted to note that he brought his change of clothes slung over his left arm and carried his toothpaste and toothbrush in his hand.

My English father, on the other hand, makes lists about what he's going to be packing weeks in advance and folds his clothes neatly in tidy suitcases.

But I digress. Which, as we have established, is genetic.

I've known Barb since our sons were in kindergarten. Soon after we met, Barb and I took our four very young kids camping. Our tent was destroyed in a hail storm and we had a close encounter with a bear. We've been friends ever since. More like family, really.

When you live in another country from the family you grew up with, friends like Barb and Craig and their children become even more important, perhaps. We've spent Christmases and

Thanksgivings together, playing cards and spending the whole day in our pajamas. Our kids love one another. Their family met and loved Bhima.

There's a familiarity about Barb and Craig. A goodness.

As we walk around the cranberry bog, Barb tells me about her kids and her mom and her sister and for a couple of days I am thinking of something other than Bhima.

Barb's hair is springy and blonde, she's sensitive and kind and inordinately fond of dogs that no one else wants or likes.

Like Halie, who was a piebald hound dog who howled like a coyote, drooled over the furniture, and rushed at people as they entered the house. Barb tried to sound cross with her, especially when Halie ate Craig's dinner—she was particularly fond of steak and mashed potatoes—but Halie continued to do as she pleased until the day she died, with eyes for no one but Barb.

When Halie died, eventually, Barb pined for weeks.

Then she started training Seeing Eye dogs, and when, oddly, one of them didn't quite make the cut, she got to keep him.

So now my friend has the most beautiful, well-behaved pedigreed lab in America.

Peace. Normality. Ordinary life. No trauma.

Barb shares my love of early rising and fully understands that's the real reason I no longer choose to make my living as a stand-up comic. I'm so much happier going to bed when the sun sets and getting up as it's rising. And no one wants to go to a comedy club at 7:00 a.m., apparently. Or even 7:00 p.m., come to think of it.

"Why don't you go for a swim, Ali?" Barb says one morning at 5:00 a.m.

The beach near Hyannis Port on Cape Cod has white sand and a lighthouse and Barb and I get up very early, and I'm swimming naked in the ocean just after sunrise.

There's a light mist on the water and an orange light on the horizon.

I'm on my back, looking up at the sky. There's no one else on the beach, apart from my friend sitting next to her dog by the stones.

I'm in the water for a long time, swimming.

Breathing in and out. In and out.

Left, right. Left, right.

And suddenly, I have a sense of Bhima swimming next to me.

Only instead of needing his orange life vest, he is swimming on his own.

And instead of being 133 pounds with thin arms, he's at least 170 and his arms look strong and he's moving skillfully and fast through the water and he is deeply happy.

And then he is the water and the sunlight on the water and it's as if he has not left at all.

And when I leave my friends and drive home, there's Bhima sitting at my kitchen table. And he appears to be halfway through the Sunday *New York Times* crossword!

"Where did you manage to get a *New York Times* on a Sunday evening?" I blurt out.

Bhima looks up, his eyes twinkling.

"Is that really your first question, baby?"

Soon our combined laughter fills the room as the church bells from St. Paul's chime in the background.

CHAPTER 41

"Why did it take you six weeks to come to me?" I ask Bhima. "I think it has something to do with needing to be fully there before I could be here at the same time."

"Where?"

Bhima either doesn't hear my question or chooses not to answer.

We're drinking tea. Well, I am. I boiled the water in the kettle I bought for Bhima two months after we met. I've become particularly fond of Bengal spice with a little stevia in it.

"No milk?" Bhima says, surprised.

"Not today."

Suddenly, I realize I am very tired, so I head upstairs and fall into the first full night's sleep I've had since Bhima died.

✻ ✻ ✻

It's early fall in Stockbridge. The leaves are starting to turn, and in the evenings there's a chill in the air.

"Alison," Bhima says, a few days after his reappearance, as we're sitting on my deck looking out over Stockbridge. "It's time to build on what we started and get in the best physical shape of your life."

"I don't have time to exercise," I say.

He raises his eyebrows in mock horror.

"I haven't been able to concentrate on work at all since you died," I say, "I've got to get back to it! I'm supporting two kids for God's sake. Plus, I can't bear the thought of working out in a mask in a gym full of stale winter air. I need to breathe."

"Then go outside. Come on, Alison. 'Just Do It!'"

"I forgot how dictatorial you can be," I say.

I had heard about this aspect of Bhima, but only experienced it once while he was alive. I'm not sure why. Maybe after knowing me for five minutes he figured out that telling me what to do would be a mistake.

Nicole told me that when they were in India and Bhima entered a room, his siblings and cousins and the young people treated him with tremendous awe. That many Indian families treat the first-born male like a god.

"It had to be Bhima's way or the highway. It was one of the reasons it didn't work out between us," Nicole told me once.

Not with me. The one time Bhima attempted that, I broke up with him. Or tried to.

We were on a beach in the tiny village of Sitges in Spain, about an hour south of Barcelona, renting the stone house of my friend and TV comedy co-writer Lucy Shuttleworth. The magical light from the place had filled us, literally and figuratively. We'd made love all morning and we were both sad to be leaving.

It was sunny but windy, so we had eaten our sandwiches under the shelter of a large rock on a cove. We got up to go and Bhima said, "Alison? Where's the top to the water bottle?"

"I don't know," I said.

"You should find it!"

"I've been looking, and it's disappeared," I said.

"You should pay more attention to these things, Alison! Let's go," he said, in the way you might talk to a dog.

I walked away, suddenly realizing that Bhima and I were not going to work out. It was a shame, but he was obviously a dictator and I certainly wasn't going to be with a dictator.

I walked up the hill and looked out over the Mediterranean with tears in my eyes. I'm seven years old again and Dad is apoplectic with fury because I've put my bottle of chocolate milk in the fridge without a top on it. Or lost the plastic cover to the Salli Terri CD he lent me. Or left random toys on the top of my dresser when I tried to clean my room. "You spilled your water all over the table!" Dad is saying. "You're an idiot!"

"What is it, Alison?" Bhima said, when he found me.

He said it so kindly, I burst into tears. What a shame. I loved him. But . . .

"This isn't working, Bhima."

"What isn't?"

"THIS isn't. We aren't. US."

Bhima looked perplexed.

"What is wrong?"

"I'm not an idiot!" I say.

"I didn't say you were."

"Ah, but you spoke to me as if you thought I was an idiot, and that's the same thing."

Bhima looked amused.

"It's not funny."

"Alison, I really don't think we should break up over this."

"Then you have to promise me you won't try to tell me what to do. And that you'll never—ever—ever speak to me like that again."

"I promise," Bhima said, seriously.

Then he held out his arms and I walked into them.

And he kept his promise.

But now he's dead, the rules have changed apparently, and he's bossing me about like there's no tomorrow.

Which there isn't. At least, not for Bhima and me.

And now, instead of resisting his advice, which may or may not be coming from him, here I am doing exactly what Bhima is telling me to do.

But a part of me already knows that I need to listen very, very carefully if I'm going to find a way through.

CHAPTER 42

I sometimes wonder if there are more deaths than usual in our community. Or if the reason I hear about so many is because I live in a small town and everyone knows everyone and everything, pretty much.

I mean, maybe if we still lived in LA or London or New Jersey the same number of people would be dying, only we wouldn't know them?

And why is it that it seems to be the really good people who had so very much to give the world who die early? Why can't the horrible ones die instead? Like Vladimir Putin, for example?

"I can think of a few others," Bhima says darkly.

"So can I," I say. Then, "If you're in a field, which flowers do you pick first? Is that it?"

"I don't know."

I glower at him. Then I decide to tell him something I never told him when he was alive.

"Death has never felt like an ending to me," I say. "I mean, I had an unusual view of death long before I met you. I wonder . . ."

"What?"

"I wonder if my experience with the people who died in our community was in some way a preparation for what happened with us?"

"Which people?"

"I didn't tell you when you were alive because you were so literal. You would have dismissed it all as coincidence."

"Tell me now."

"EDEN KEND, Age 10

"Eden was a ten-year-old sprite with short brown hair and brown eyes who seemed much older than her years.

"It was June 25, 2016. I'd taken my then-thirteen-year-old daughter Lucy and her friend Cassie shopping in Northampton for the day. Something I did because they wanted me to, not because I like to shop. Actually I hate it."

"This I already know. Carry on," Bhima says.

"Lucy, Cassie, and I came home to my little house in Stockbridge and, after eating some watermelon and drinking some lemonade, we sat down in the sitting room. It was just before four o'clock in the afternoon, and for no reason, I heard myself saying, 'Let's sing a round! How about "White Coral Bells?" Does anyone know that?'

"'I do,' Cassie said.

"And there we were sitting on the floor of my living room singing 'White Choral Bells' in a round. I remember the purity of the sound and a curious sense of peace.

"As we sang, I remember hearing the church clock strike four.

"The next morning Cassie's mother arrived, pale, in shock and told us that little Eden had died. Suddenly, while playing tag with her cousins.

"Lucy and Cassie had known Eden well. They both screamed. Then Cassie fainted. We picked her up, gave her some water, then without saying a word we all drove straight to Eden's mother's house where friends and family were gathering, in shock, to be with Diane, whose husband was not yet there.

"Diane, a naturally joyous spirit, was sitting on a bench, under a tree.

"I hugged her. Then for some reason I said, 'Lucy, Cassie and I have been singing White Choral Bells in a round.'

"Diane laughed. 'Did you know that was Eden's favorite song?'

"'I did not,' I said. Then 'When, exactly, did Eden die?'

"'At four o'clock yesterday afternoon,' Diane said."

"LOUISA, Age 14

"Then there was Louisa, who drowned off the coast of Rhode Island at age fourteen when she was snorkelling with her father.

"We all knew her—my kids did parkour with her, a cool kind of gymnastics that involved running up walls and doing somersaults mid-air—all part of my campaign to keep my son taking healthy risks in a community where many kids, boys in particular, were getting high by the age of eleven. Over my dead body was my son going down that path. We found parkour instead and that's how we became friends with Louisa.

"And then we heard about Louisa on the news.

"'Rhode Island—A teenager died Wednesday (July 15) after going missing for several hours in the rough waters off Rhode Island.'

"The entire community was in shock.

"A couple of days later I drove up to Boothbay Harbour in Maine for the annual AudioFile Magazine Lobsterbake. And on the way home to Stockbridge I stayed with a friend near Cape Cod, got up before dawn and on a whim asked Siri to take me to the nearest beach.

"There's a heavy mist and I'm walking on the beach at 6:00 a.m. past some rocks, thinking about Louisa when I see a beautiful, golden pink light above the ocean. It's sunrise, but there's something more to it than any sunrise I've seen before or since. It was brighter somehow. Hard to describe.

"Suddenly, I have a sense of Louisa up there in the sky, floating way up high, above the rocks to my left. She's filled with the light that's coming through the clouds. And then so am I. My heart is filled with something beautiful. It feels like love and light.

"Louisa's asking me to call her grandmother and tell her 'everything is alright. I'm transitioning.'

"'Transitioning'? Not a word I'm familiar with in any context. Huh?

"But I do as I am told and call Louisa's grandmother Andrea and convey the message.

"And after a moment's pause, Andrea says, 'thank you.'"

"ADRIAN, Age 18

"Adrian was a beautiful human being and a star athlete. He was killed by a drunk driver when he was walking on campus at Amherst College at the age of nineteen. After he died, I saw his mother, Julienne, a gifted musician, in a bookshop. She had a glow about her—a grace and radiance. I met her again at Kripalu in 2019 and we stood talking for two hours. For some reason I asked about Adrian and she told me everything—all about how he had died, and what it was like visiting him when he was unconscious in Albany Medical Center."

"He died in the Albany Medical Center too?" Bhima says.

"Yes."

"Dreadful lighting in there. And they really should do something about those lumpy pillows."

"NICK, Age 70

"Nick was the grandfather of Louisa. He had Parkinson's. His wife, Andrea, invited me to see him as she said she didn't think he had long to live.

"When I got there, I asked him if he wanted to write something about his life. He said he couldn't because of the shakes. So I suggested I ask him questions and record his answers. Then we could transcribe the conversation and he'd have a book.

"Nick was energized by the idea and lived for another year. And in that year I would go over most Saturdays, ask him questions about his life, and record his answers on his iPhone.

"It eventually became a very short book which we called *Conversations with Nick* and distributed amongst his family and friends after he died.

"One of the questions I asked him was, 'If you could give three pieces of advice to the people you leave behind what would they be?'

"And he said, 'That's easy. Love is the only thing that matters. Remember, people are doing the best they can with who they are. And connect, because it is only in connection that love can find expression.'

"Is that the guy you quoted at my funeral?" Bhima says.

"Yes."

CHAPTER 43

Bhima hands me an article from *The Berkshire Eagle.*
"Say goodbye to boring treadmill work and forge a heartier spirit with every adventure," the article says.

Since the pandemic started, Mike Bassillion, a supremely fit fifty-year-old American who loves football, basketball, and other things about America that I find perplexing, has started leading outdoor training and hikes through something called Berkshire Adventure Fitness.

And so, towards the end of 2020, with the gyms shut down by the pandemic, I'm following Mike with my fellow hikers through the Berkshire landscape like a line of ducklings.

We hike up Laura's Tower, Monument Mountain, and Flag Rock with weights on our backs, something Mike calls "rucking." We lift sandbags as we walk around the Housatonic Flats. We do push-ups and lunges at Thomas & Palmer Brook.

And whenever I feel tired, I hear Bhima's voice saying, "Keep going, Alison! Stop phoning it in!"

I push myself harder. As I do, my body grows stronger.

And on the days I am not working out with Mike, I run through the stunning property owned by the Marian Fathers that looks out over Stockbridge and beyond. I turn left on Larrywaug Crossing, then onto Route 102. I run along the famous path with trees on either side of it, leading up to a sign saying "Closed to the Public Until Further Notice."

I run through the graveyard where Mumbet is buried. She was an enslaved African woman who sued for her freedom based on "All Men Are Created Free and Equal" and won. She is buried in the same plot as her attorney, the great, great, great something-or-other grandfather of the actress Kyra Sedgewick, who will probably lie there one day with her husband Kevin Bacon on whom I have always had a crush.

I spent a lifetime avoiding love because I was so afraid of losing it. Now I've lost it; why do I feel more alive than ever?

I realize I am acutely aware of everything. The smell of rain on the earth. The shape of the clouds. Light in light.

The fact that people all over the world are losing loved ones, some of them in far worse ways.

Bhima died in his prime. When he was very much in love. After a perfect day. He didn't have to watch his brain or body get sick or old.

"And I didn't have to come back from my coma with half my brain," Bhima says.

"You would have hated that."

"I would. And as for you!"

"Me?"

"What kind of life would it have been for you, Alison? I mean, you'd be a terrible nurse."

"I'd have found a way."

"Sure. But you'd have been miserable, baby."

Where's the despair?

Is it over there. Is it coming?

Instead of wanting to hide under the bed and never come out again, I'm wanting to do the opposite. I'm filled with an extra energy—a kind of deep joy that I don't understand.

I keep thinking about the words Desmond Tutu said to me: "I can't control what happens to me. But I can control how I respond to it."

Our mutual friend and my one-time agent Lynn Franklin says, "Why don't you write to Desmond Tutu and tell him what happened?" And I say, "I can't take up his time, he's a busy guy!" And she says, "No, he kept tabs on you and he loved you and he'd want to know."

SO I made myself write him a short email and I told him I'd spent a lifetime avoiding love because I was so afraid of the worst happening. But then, when I fell in love, and the worst did happen, instead of wanting to crawl under the bed and never come out again, I find I want to live and love—more fully than ever. What IS that?

He didn't answer my question but he did write back and said, "Alison, first of all I want you to know I have asked God to find you another soul mate. And She said She is on the case. But first, you must do everything within your power to make sure this story is told as widely as possible." I wrote back saying, "I can't bear to write another book," and he said, "So tell jokes, sing songs—whatever—but tell it!"

And there you were with your arms crossed and throwing your head back, laughing, saying, "You can't ignore Archbishop Desmond Tutu. Just Bloody Do It!"

CHAPTER 44

The phone rings.

"Hi, Mom," Tom says. "I'm coming home for a few days."

Excellent. There's no more legitimate reason to put off writing than the return of one of your children.

Even Bhima has to admit that when Tom's home there isn't time or room to think about much else.

Tom is charismatic as all get-out and has a lot to say and as all of it is interesting, people—including me—tend to get caught up in a bit of a whirlwind when Tom's around. Six-foot-four, talented, unpredictable, connected, kind. Vulnerable.

It's been just Bhima and me. Now the space will be filled with Tom.

I'll need to make a shift.

I mustn't cry. I don't want to worry him.

During the pandemic, Tom learned how to cook and look after himself, staying near his school in Savannah rather than putting his parents at risk for COVID.

He seems different somehow.

"No one in Savannah cares about the pandemic," Tom says, looking around at all the anxious New Englanders wearing masks. "This paranoia is crazy."

Maybe it is. Who knows?

Tom thinks he's immortal, of course. He's twenty. He's young. COVID without a vaccine hasn't hurt him. It would have killed Bhima.

Now for the first time, I'm aware that if Bhima had lived, we would have had to quarantine frequently to protect him. Bhima would have hated that.

At first I assumed Tom would be immune to COVID because he's so tall. Which, to my logic, meant the germs would be flying around a foot below his nose and mouth, so he wouldn't get it.

But Tom's had COVID twice so far. And despite the fact that he was at high risk because of a spontaneous pneumothorax, the worst did not happen and he not only didn't die, he appears to be stronger than he has ever been.

I turn my back to Tom as I add pepper to the spaghetti sauce.

"Why are you crying, Mom?" Tom says, somehow figuring it out.

"Because Bhima and I made this sauce together," I say. "And . . ."

Suddenly I can't hold it in. And the boy I held in my arms for the first few years of his life is holding me in his.

Up until this point in my life I've hidden my vulnerability from my kids, with some success.

"I'm sorry this happened, Mom. I really liked Bhima," Tom says.

I blow my nose loudly.

"Sorry," I say.

"Don't be sorry, Mom. Geez! You're so British!"

Then, later, as we're sitting on the couch, I say, "Everything okay at school?"

"It's all good," Tom says, tossing a pretzel into his mouth and missing.

There are pretzels all over the sofa, actually. Which would infuriate Tom's father, and Bhima for that matter, but doesn't bother me at all.

Come to think of it, where is Bhima?

"Is everything okay?" I ask Tom again.

"Yes. I came home to check on you, Mom. Plus . . ."

"Yes?"

"I wanted to thank you."

"What for?"

"For all those years of putting your own life on hold and working real real hard to get me to the school I needed. For putting up with my attitude, which I know wasn't great. . ."

"Ya think?" I say, laughing.

"Mom, I'm real happy now and every decision you made helped get me here. So thanks. And . . ."

"And?"

"I know how happy you were with Bhima. And you were lucky to find him. But he was real lucky to find you."

His kindness sets me off crying again.

"Are you okay?" Tom asks again as he's leaving.

"I will be," I tell him. "I promise."

CHAPTER 45

"So are you going to start writing now?" Bhima says, when Tom's left.

"I'm not sure I can bear to go back and relive it all . . ."

"Do you think the Arch thought, 'Oh great! Can't wait to spend another day listening to the terrible stories at the Truth and Reconciliation Commission in South Africa?' If a guy like that, who's devoted his entire life to helping people, asks you to do something, you do it."

I know.

"I'm not ignoring him. I just have no idea where to start."

"Well, what do you always tell writers when they don't know what to write about?"

I sigh.

"If you could only say one thing, what would it be?"

I know full well that once I start thinking about the story, I'll become immersed in it. And I'll have no choice but to drop everything else until it is done.

"So what are you going to write first?" Bhima asks. "A show or a book?"

"With a show, the audience is with you every night and you can hear them responding to what you're saying. With a book you have no idea if people like it or not. Or find the parts of it that you find hilarious even remotely funny."

"So write a show!" Bhima says.

"If it's a solo show, it's just me on stage. I don't want to do this on my own."

Cross, I climb into bed and, with Bhima next to me in the shape of my pillow, I eventually fall asleep.

I wake up suddenly at 5:00 a.m.

"What does 'Ubuntu' mean?" I say.

Bhima, who is lying next to me this morning, groans. Bhima has never been fond of my early morning revelations. He mumbles, "Google it," before turning over and going back to sleep.

Bleary-eyed, I reach for my glasses, turn on my laptop, and type in "Ubuntu."

Of course! Lo and behold, Google is quoting the Arch.

"One of the sayings in our country is 'Ubuntu'—the essence of being human. In other words, I am not an island. I am only a person through other people."

Not sure what that means.

"Go back to sleep," Bhima mumbles.

I do fall back to sleep. And I dream of Archbishop Desmond Tutu again.

I see him speaking to a large crowd with the energy and authority of an Old Testament prophet.

Then I see him alone, in a small room, wrapped in a blanket, praying.

I hear his words. They come to me lightly in a dream.

"So write songs, tell jokes, whatever. But tell this story, Alison."

And then that word again.

"Ubuntu."

When I wake up, I know exactly what to do.

I'll call Gary.

CHAPTER 46

If you think you don't know Gary Schreiner, actually you probably do. He's an Emmy-Award-winning composer who's
worked with everyone from Joan Osborne to Sting. He's played
in bars, clubs, the Carlton Club, my living room, and Carnegie
Hall.

Gary wrote the music for my first show and he's my son's
godfather, despite the fact that he is Jewish. He showed up to
Tom's christening in LA dressed in traditional Chinese clothing
(he was married to a Chinese woman at the time.) And we've
always been creatively in sync.

"How are you holding up?" Gary asks.

"I'm okay. And I've got an idea."

"Just one?" Gary starts laughing. We know each other very
well.

"If I were to write another solo show—"

"Yes," Gary says, without waiting to hear the rest of the
question. Then, "What's it called, Alison?"

"How about *Grief . . . A Comedy*"?

"I'm in."

I get in my car and, for the first time since Bhima died, I
leave my house and drive to New York.

The city is still reeling from the pandemic. The homeless
population has tripled. People who have been shut up in their
apartments are out on the streets now, but they're wearing masks.
The horror stories of countless dead bodies are winding down a
bit, but you can tell the city has been hurt.

Gary has been making music by Zoom, mostly, but he's a
social guy and it hasn't been easy.

I haven't seen Gary in two years. He's happy to see me, and, as usual, very opinionated about where I should park my car.

So opinionated, he won't let me park without him.

So I have to stop outside his building on 145th Street and Broadway to pick him up and he hops in.

As anyone who has watched *Seinfeld* can testify, in NYC you get alternate side of the street parking on Mondays and Thursdays. At 11:00 a.m. It is 11:05. I've already driven two and a half hours to get here and I need to pee. I would have no problem paying for parking.

But Gary IS Jerry Seinfeld, with a touch of George from time to time. There is no way he is going to allow this.

"Don't be so nice," he says as I stop the car at a crosswalk. "Drive through the people. They'll scatter, like pigeons."

At Gary's insistence, I speed down 165th to Riverside Drive, turn right and right again. Around the block. And around the block. And around the block.

Ninety minutes later, we find a parking space.

"See?" Gary says, triumphantly. "Told you we'd find a spot. We can see your car from my window! You won't have to move it for two days."

Gary and I met thirty years ago, when one of his many female Friends With Benefits brought him to see me as a rookie stand-up comic performing at Gladys' Comedy Club—which was basically a tiny platform with a mic, situated at the far end of a fish restaurant.

Playing to a handful of people in a restaurant that smelled of fish and had a low-hanging cottage cheese ceiling from when it used be an office was a challenge for everyone. But if you could get a laugh at Gladys' you could get a laugh anywhere.

I'd develop new material at Gladys' Comedy Club and take whatever worked to The Comic Strip or Carolines. Every comic passed through there—Darryl Hammond, Greg Giraldo. Jim Gaffigan and I were on the same lineup the night O.J. Simpson was being chased by cops along the LA highway on a TV screen just to the left of the stage.

I was living in Nyack at the time, twenty miles north of New York City, in the house the writer Carson McCullers turned into apartments at the advice of Tennessee Williams, who turned

to her one day and said, "Writers never make any money, but
landladies do. Why don't you buy a house, turn it into apartments,
and live in one yourself?"

Later, Carson had an affair with her female psychiatrist and
then left her the house. She was my landlady.

The first time Gary came to see me in Nyack with the friend
who introduced us, we put on *Mary Poppins* and skipped around my
basement apartment singing "Supercalefragelisticexpialedocious."

We became instant friends.

It's a relief to be with Gary again, in an old, familiar world.
I've been so very far away. Gary never actually met Bhima, but he
heard a lot about him.

Gary and I push open the doors leading from the busy
street outside into his apartment building and head up the
broken marble stairs with black edging. Gary's place has wooden
floors and a fish tank and a Food Museum, which began when
he discovered his fondness for peculiar food items that he came
across when traveling. Like One Whole Chicken in Can, Ma
Ling Brandough, and Orthodox Chews.

"Got any lyrics?" Gary says once we're upstairs.

"Yup."

"What sort of feel?" he says, while filling up the cats' dish
with water.

"Maybe the same vibe as the theme tune to *M*A*S*H*?"

I grab a handful of cashews and follow Gary into his studio.
He's already sitting at the keyboard.

We write the song in under half an hour.

We hang.

Then we watch *Judge Judy*, because Gary never misses it.

I feel strangely calm and am lulled to sleep by the familiar
sounds of New York blaring outside Gary's spare room window.

The next day we have breakfast, listen to music, play with
the cats, and talk to Gary's girlfriend, Jennifer, on the phone.

Soon we are laying down a rough track, which takes longer
than usual because I have to stop to cry every so often.

Jennifer is a grief counselor and she'd warned Gary that
tears were likely. So Gary has come prepared with a fresh box
of Kleenex and waits patiently each time until I'm ready to sing

again.

The next day I hurry back home so I can be alone with Bhima.

In the car, I listen to the demo tape of me singing the first song I've written in years.

"Don't waste your time on things that you know really aren't worth a dime.

"Each day you get to choose how you will spend it.

"Don't waste a minute 'cos tonight might end it.

"Don't waste your time."

Gary has helped me catch it—a little bit of this emerging revelation. This knowing. A little bit of what the Arch is asking me to communicate.

CHAPTER 47

"What about the other thing Archbishop Desmond Tutu talked about?"

"Oh, that."

"Yes, that."

I look at Bhima and hold out my hand. I imagine him taking my palm to his mouth and kissing it. Softly.

"Tell me again," Bhima says.

"The Arch said to Lynn, 'Now that Alison has lost her man, I have asked God to find her another soulmate. And God said She is on the case.' Then Lynn said to me, 'When the Arch puts you on his prayer list, you're on it for life.'"

"Do you think a man like the Arch forgets the people on his prayer list after he dies?" Bhima says.

"Probably not."

"Neither do I. It's been NINE MONTHS, Alison. You've seen your coffee shop buddies and the few friends who pushed so hard that you couldn't turn them down. And Gary. Otherwise you've been alone."

"I haven't been alone. I've been with you!"

Today, for some reason, Bhima's wearing a tweed jacket and smoking a pipe. He looks like an Indian Sherlock Holmes.

He is pacing up and down the gold Oriental rug that I bought because it reminded me of the one that traveled with our family from Washington, D.C., to Kenya to the Ivory Coast and eventually back to our sitting room in England again.

"You need to come out of hiding if you're going to find love again."

"I'm not in hiding!"

"You are. And given that you live in the middle of nowhere, I think we should start with online dating. It worked for me several times."

"And look where that got you," I say darkly.

I list off the names of the last few women Bhima met online with whom he was mostly miserable.

"It's alright," I say gently. "Neither of us knew what we should have been holding out for. And every time, you were determined to do everything you could to make things work."

"Yes. But being with the wrong person meant I wasn't available to be with the right person. I had no idea of the difference. Until I met you," Bhima says.

"We didn't have long," I whisper.

"It was long enough. And if it was me, I'd be out there already looking for it again."

"I won't find *you* again."

"No. But you'll find love again. And now that you know what the real thing feels like, you won't settle for anything else.

"SO . . ." he says, bringing up Match.com, taking me by the hand and sitting me down at the computer. "At least take a look."

I do look. For a whole hour. At men holding up dead fish— what is that? Am I missing something? I mean seriously, am I? Men on motorbikes. Men with tattoos. Men with fancy cars. All online in the hope of finding love or sex or some kind of connection. The soulmate-seekers. The wife-seekers. The lover-seekers. The sex-with-no-strings-attached-seekers. All hoping they'll find what Bhima and I found, by taking a shot in the dark.

"I can't, Bhima!" I say.

Later, Bhima says, "By the way, do you remember the local matchmaker you signed up with before you met me?

"Marcie the Matchmaker?"

"The very same. Well, she wrote to tell you how sorry she was to hear about my death. I've emailed her back on your behalf thanking her for her kindness. I also told her you're ready to meet people again."

"But I'm not!"

"She wants you to fill out a profile."

I am sitting with my arms firmly crossed, glaring at him.

Unperturbed, Bhima turns back to the laptop and starts typing.

Uh-oh.

"No, Bhima!"

"Write your own profile then," he says, raising his hands.

Very clever.

"Alright, what's my status?" I ask Bhima.

"Widow."

I type, "Widow." Then, "What do I write next?"

"Try the truth!"

The truth. Okay then. What IS the truth? I mean, what is it really?

I start to type.

Alison

Age: 56

Summary: I am looking for a smart, funny, kind, interesting chemical engineer from South India with a passion for actually doing something about climate change, who went to R.P.I. and is totally trustworthy, who I love and who knows how to love me back.

"Alisonnnnnn." Bhima can't help laughing.

He looks at me for a long moment. Then, gently, he says, "You sleep so much better when you are not alone."

I look back at him for about a minute.

And then—eureka!

"You're right!" I say.

"I am?"

"You are! I know exactly what to do."

Bhima is looking at me with suspicion.

"I do sleep better when I'm sleeping with another mammal. But it doesn't necessarily have to have two legs."

❉ ❉ ❉

"Ali," Barb says, a few days after I told her who I was looking for, "I've found your dog! He's a dachshund who has just been rescued from an Amish puppy mill."

"An AMISH puppy mill?" Bhima says.

"An AMISH puppy mill?" I say.

"Yeah, I know. He's totally mistrustful of humans. They're farmers who kept him in a cage for three years and never let him out. They hosed down the cage and treated him like a farm animal. He's never even been on grass, let alone a leash. They were going to kill him because he'd stopped eating, which was when the rescue guy stepped in. They want him to be adopted by someone who will be home a lot, who'll have time to work with him, and who 'gets' trauma."

"That's you!" Bhima says.

Four hours later, I'm peering through the wire of a crate at a miniature tan dachshund cowering in the corner.

"Hallo, Charlie," I say, softly.

He slowly turns his head toward me. I can see how badly he's been hurt.

I also recognize the glimmer of hope in his eyes.

"It's okay," I say. "I've got you."

He walks hesitatingly toward me, sniffs my hand, and then allows me to pick him up. I put the little dog into a soft gray sling and his head rests against my chest for the next few hours.

When I take Charlie out of the sling, he smells grass for the first time.

In the beginning he eats only from my hand. Then he eats from a bowl.

At first he's passive and lies on his back with his paws in the air waiting for me to pick him up. Then, gradually, he begins to follow me about the house.

He sits on my lap while I'm driving.

He comes down to the coffee shop with me in the mornings and peers at the Bobs from the sling and the safety of my lap, listening to the conversation, receiving compliments and dog biscuits.

Soon he is hiking with me up Monument Mountain, growling at men in hats if they have the temerity to come within ten feet of me.

When I do push-ups, Charlie clambers on my back to check for predators.

When I get into bed at night, Charlie lies with his head on

my neck as we drift off to sleep. If I awaken in the night, I find the little tan dog has positioned himself right next to me with his long back pressed against mine.

In the mornings he burrows under the comforter Bhima and I slept under, refusing to get up until he is good and ready.

With Charlie in my life, I no longer wake in the dark of the night screaming.

CHAPTER 48

Bhima is Googling dating sites again.

Charlie looks up from the couch and trots over to me so I can pick him up and sit with him in my arms. He licks my face, then curls his long body into a ball with a sigh and dozes off on my lap.

"Alison, Charlie is cute, but I'm not going to let you spend the rest of your life with your arms around your dachshund, like Niobe, all tears, smiling at grief."

Is that Bhima misquoting *Twelfth Night?* Or is it me?

"What are you afraid of?" Bhima asks.

"Before I met you, I'd stay with a man even when I realized he wasn't right for me."

"Because he was too old or depressed or a strain to talk to?"

"Right."

"So why didn't you just leave when you found out they weren't the right fit?"

"For the same reason you stayed with your girlfriends."

"Because you liked them and didn't want to hurt their feelings?"

"Exactly!"

Silence. Stillness.

I remember Bhima telling me he was about to break up with a girl when she told him she'd been abused for years as a child. "I couldn't break up with her after that," Bhima said.

They were together for the next twelve years.

"And you were unhappy, so you stayed very very busy," I said.

"I raced cars at Lime Rock. I rode my motorcycle at top speed all over the country. I pushed myself hard and did well in my work. I didn't know you were in the world. I didn't know . . ."

Eventually the girl left him and Bhima moved to Vermont.

"Meeting each other was a kind of miracle, wasn't it?" we whisper at the same time.

Bhima takes my hands and pulls me to my feet. I can almost hear the most beautiful music I have ever heard. Almost. And as I move with Bhima standing right in front of me, my fear is replaced by warmth that floods my heart and every part of my being.

Now I can feel my beloved's cheek pressed against mine as I breathe in. Then out. Then in. Then out again.

A little later, we're sitting at the kitchen table when Bhima says, "You will go out and meet people. You will give them a fair chance. But the moment your knower tells you that you could never love them, you will swiftly extricate yourself from the situation, so you can be free to find true love again. You will not get stuck in a relationship that is wrong because you don't want to hurt someone's feelings or because you are lonely."

"How will I know?"

"I will help you. I won't let you make a mistake on this one, baby."

"So, what are you going to do, come on the dates with me?" I say.

Bhima grins. "Something like that."

"Are you going to turn down the radiator in the bedroom so it doesn't clang all night?" Bhima says later as I'm cleaning my teeth.

"Just a minute!"

I spit the toothpaste into the drain that doesn't have a plug—why, I have no idea. Another missing top of a kind.

I head to the old steel gray radiators.

Which way do I need to twist the knob to turn this off? That's right. Righty Tighty, Lefty Loosey.

That night I dream I'm in a cave, resting with someone I can't see, in the center of the earth. We're lying on a rug made of some kind of animal skin laid out on a dark gray rock. The air is warm and sweet.

We are curled up together in the semi-darkness with a thin ray of golden light illuminating small particles of dust through a crack in the cave.

CHAPTER 49

One sunny morning the actor/producer Jim Frangione appears at my back door on his electric bike.

Jim works a lot with David Mamet. He set up a local theatre company called Great Barrington Public Theater who produce new work. He's been trying to get me to write something for them for years.

"Any ideas for another solo show yet, Alison?"

"Yes!" I say.

Jim's eyes light up.

"What?"

"What do you think of the title? *Grief... A Comedy*."

Jim starts to laugh. Then he laughs longer.

Then Jim says, "Great. I'll produce the first incarnation. Let's do a run of it in June."

"I've got a song or two, but I haven't even started the script yet."

"No problem," Jim says. "I know you can do it. We'll produce it in June."

Then, before I can respond, he's biking toward the Big Y to pick up some milk, cheese, and Kombucha before heading home.

Only in the Berkshires.

❋   ❋   ❋

I'm writing down some ideas in the notepad I keep by the side of my bed. Charlie has burrowed under the blankets, as is his wont, and is curled up, fast asleep, between my feet.

Bhima is sitting at the end of the bed, stroking the cat,

looking out the window at the sky.

Ping.

You Have A Match!

"The matchmaker has matched you with a guy called Ted Thomas," Bhima says, beyond excited. "Come on, Alison. Let's take a look at his profile."

Name: Ted Thomas
Age: 58
Race: white
Ed.: MBA
Beliefs: spiritual
Politics: progressive
Height: 6'4"
Body size: average
Hair: blond
Divorced with one son
Employed: >$75,000 a year, environmentalist
Creative, reliable, humorous, nurturing, resilient, diplomatic
Interests: Reading, music, Scottish dancing, environment, gardening, hiking, yoga, kayaking, cooking, working out, snow-shoeing.

"He's into renewable energy," Bhima says, reading on.

I look over Bhima's shoulder and read the rest of Ted's profile with him.

"And he's a fan of Gilbert and Sullivan!" I say.

"Who?"

Dad was brought up on Gilbert and Sullivan, and, as a result, so was I.

A memory jumps in. Of Dad and I singing together—to the frequent annoyance of the rest of the family, who would rather we didn't.

I used to get the mad laughs whenever Dad changed the lyrics.

On a tree by a willow a little Tom Tit
Sang willow, tit willow, tit willow.
And I said to him, "Dicky bird, why do you shit,
Singing Willow, tit willow, tit willow . . ."

"Alison!" Bhima says, interrupting my thoughts. "Look! Ted is into Scottish dancing too. Like your parents."

"Yes."

I read on.

"You know him, Bhima! You're linked on LinkedIn."

"I don't think I know, know him. But we may have met at an environmental conference at some point."

I feel a shoot of adrenaline.

Gilbert and Sullivan AND Scottish dancing AND renewable energy AND a link to Bhima?

Is Ted the soulmate the Arch said he would pray for?

CHAPTER 50

Ted and I arrange to meet in a field in Lenox. It's still the pandemic, so we can't meet inside. Our plan is to go for a walk.

Bhima and I wait in the parking lot. Bhima is wearing his gray flannel jacket. I am in my light green anorak, a light blue scarf, jeans, and sneakers.

As Ted gets out of the car Bhima says, "Oh, my god! He's a giant!"

The man is big. Six-foot-five. Huge by Indian standards.

In his profile Ted said he was fifty-eight. But this man can't be a day under seventy-five.

"He lied about his age!" Bhima says. "Don't waste your time. Let's go."

Ted is walking slowly toward us. He's dressed like Dad would be if he were here. He has on a corduroy cap and a tweed jacket.

"He looks sweet," I say. "Plus, he's come all the way from Connecticut. And he looks so comforting," I say, smiling at Ted and walking toward him.

"Oh, no. Noooooo," Bhima says.

It feels nice to be walking outside with someone who feels so familiar.

Ted tells me about his work in renewable energy. The rest of the time he takes part in amateur dramatics. He played the Major General in *The Pirates of Penzance* last summer.

"I am the very model of a modern major general,

"I've information vegetable, animal, and mineral," I begin.

Before I know it we are singing Gilbert and Sullivan, then English folk songs and then Molly Malone.

I've still not been able to get home to England because of the pandemic. Singing with this man takes me there in the same way narrating classic English audiobooks takes me there. I feel a sense of homecoming.

He's been divorced for five years, has a son, a vegetable garden, solar panels, and goes contra dancing every weekend. He is also an enthusiastic member of the AARP. When I ask him what that is, exactly, he tells me and encourages me to join.

"But I'm only fifty-six," I say. "And I'm not retired."

"You don't have to be!" he says with excitement.

After we've been walking for an hour and are heading back toward the car, Ted says, "Do you believe in premarital digital contact, Alison?"

"Huh?" Bhima says.

"I'm sorry?" I say to Ted.

Ted looks at me with a gleam in his eye and wiggles his fingers.

"Would you like to hold my hand?" Ted says.

"Premarital digital contact?" Bhima says, making a vomiting gesture to my left.

I shoot a "stop-being-so-rude" glance at Bhima.

"Alright," I say to Ted, smiling up at him.

It's a bit of a shock, but I like holding someone else's hand again.

"Alison, he's old enough to be your father!" Bhima says toward the end of our walk.

"I'd like to do this again," Ted says.

"That would be nice," I say, helping Ted into his car.

"WHAAAAAT?" Bhima says, his voice carried off in the wind.

CHAPTER 51

"You LIKE him?" Bhima says later, stunned.

"I must do. I have adrenaline running."

"Adrenaline is your body's response saying 'fight or flight.' It has to be flight, Alison. Your husband was fourteen years older than you and you were miserable. This guy is even older!"

"Sure, but Brian was a rock-and-roll drummer from New Jersey with whom I had absolutely nothing in common. Ted loves Scottish dancing and he knows about Burns Night and amateur dramatics!"

"But that was your parents' life."

"Right."

"Not the one you chose."

"Right."

"You left that life to come here."

"I did."

"You can't be attracted to Ted!"

"Why not?"

"I repeat, he's much too old for you! You've made that mistake more than once before. You can't go back to your former way of doing things. Not after all this!"

Bhima has clearly forgotten that I don't like anyone telling me what to do.

I respond to Ted's text asking to see me again in the affirmative.

Later, casually, Bhima says, "Why don't you introduce Ted to Sasha?"

"Alright," I say. "Next week. When he takes me out to lunch."

Over lunch the following Sunday, I learn that Ted is also a member of the Rotary Club, his renewable energy clients come from LinkedIn, and he knows more limericks than anyone I have ever met.

My adrenaline is still running. Bhima is probably a little jealous. Which isn't really fair, given that it's he who's been pushing me to do the dating thing in the first place.

As we leave the restaurant, before Ted takes my hand again, I say, "Let's pop in and see my friend Sasha. She's just across the road."

Sasha has been put on notice that this might happen and meets us outside, on the stone path leading to her kitchen.

Sasha is as good as I am at making people feel like a million bucks, but when Ted goes to the end of her garden to take a phone call, Sasha turns to me with concern and says, "Is he alright?"

"What do you mean?"

"He doesn't seem to have very good balance, Alison."

"He's just old," I say.

"Exactly," Sasha says.

"Exactly," Bhima says.

"You're being prejudiced," I say crossly.

"Plus," Sasha says, "is he wearing a toupée?"

"He is!" Bhima says with glee.

"What's wrong with that?" I say.

"Really?" Bhima and Sasha say in unison.

"Alison," Sasha says, "he's at least seventy-five years old. He'll be dead soon."

"Bhima was younger than me. There are no guarantees," I say, smiling at Ted, who is putting his flip phone back in his pocket.

CHAPTER 52

The following weekend, on date number three, I invite Ted to have lunch with me at my home. Ted is the first person other than my children to come into the house since the pandemic began, but he's tested negative for COVID and it is awfully cold outside.

My adrenaline is still running steadily. It has to be attraction. What else could it be?

He sits down and I begin getting salmon out of the fridge.

"This is nice," Ted says from my couch.

I look at him from the kitchen. He's taken off his shoes and has put his feet up.

"I'm glad you're comfortable," I say.

When lunch is ready Ted stands up and comes over to the dining table. Our dining table. Bhima's dining table.

"You've spilled water on the table," he says as he sits down.

"Yes," I say. "I do that. I'm a spiller."

Then he tucks into what I have to say is really delicious salmon. My friend Tony taught me how to cook it. You put the salmon in a cold oven, spread mustard on the top, turn the oven up to 450 degrees, then take it out after twenty-five minutes. And voila!

"Where's the top to the mustard?" Ted says after we've eaten.

"Uh-oh," I hear Bhima saying from somewhere close. He sounds delighted.

I am not delighted. Instead, I am feeling slightly put out that Ted hasn't said a word about how good the salmon was.

Bhima ALWAYS complimented my cooking. Even when it wasn't great. Because he was Indian. Because he was polite.

Because he knew better than to receive a meal from someone who dislikes cooking as much as I do without expressing profuse appreciation.

Ted is still looking for the top to the Dijon mustard.

Without asking, Ted gets up and opens my refrigerator door.

"There's a water bottle in here that's topless too," he says.

Bhima is grinning. I say nothing.

Will he help with the washing up?

No, it seems. He will not. Instead, he will sit on a chair telling me a very long joke about a parrot. Bhima is thrilled.

"So there's this parrot," Ted begins . . .

Oh, no.

"As a comedian you're gonna love this. It's so funny," Ted says, chuckling.

Bhima is sitting smugly in the corner with his arms crossed.

Bhima knows that one of my pet hates is people telling me jokes the moment they learn that I am a comedian. All comics get this. We don't tell jokes. But people who don't know this assume that talking to a comedian gives them carte blanche to tell their favorite joke, which is torture for comedians, who have a low boredom threshold at the best of times.

Ted is telling the joke very, very slowly.

This I cannot bear.

"Tell him now," Bhima says.

"He told me over the phone I make him happy!" I whisper to Bhima.

"Tell him!" Bhima says.

"Oh, gosh," I say suddenly to Ted, as I jump up and head for the back door. "I'm so sorry. I completely forgot! I promised I'd go and see Sasha. I'm afraid I'm going to have to go now. So sorry. Please—well, let yourself out. I'll see you soon!"

Then I smile tightly and leave the house. I can't bear to be around him any longer.

Why did I not simply ask him to leave?

Because I am still more English than American and I don't want to hurt his feelings.

To my dismay, when I return from my walk, Ted is still in

my house.

Who is this intruder? This big man taking up so much space in my little house, in my precious sanctuary? Where it's usually just me and Bhima.

I can't bear to be in the same room as Ted one moment longer. I actually think I might hate him. I want him out of my space.

"I'm so sorry Ted," I say, eventually. "But I have a lot of things to do this afternoon, so . . ."

"I think I'll take a nap before I drive," Ted says.

And before I can say anything else, Ted is fast asleep on the couch.

Our couch.

The couch Bhima and I have sat on for months and months and months. With nobody else there.

Who is this oaf?

After twenty minutes, I cough loudly to wake him up.

"I'm sorry," I say to Ted, finally. "But I have a lot to do. I'm sure you understand."

"Do you want me to leave?"

"Yes, please."

"Okay, cutie." Ted says.

Then, as he's leaving, he bends down, picks up the top to the mustard, which suddenly appears on the chair where Bhima was sitting, opens the fridge, puts it on the mustard jar, pinches my cheek and winks at me.

"I'll see you soon," he says, waving goodbye.

I go inside and start typing the email.

Dear Ted,

You are a lovely person, but I am sorry to say I don't think we are a compatible match.

I wish you nothing but the best,

Alison

And the moment I press send, the adrenaline stops.

"I hate hurting his feelings," I say to Bhima, later. "He's a sweet man. Just all wrong for me."

"I know. But it's better to tell him as soon as you know. Before the poor bastard falls head over heels in love with you."

"Yes."

I'm perplexed by the bottles without tops. I could have sworn I put the lid back on the mustard last night.

"Did you have anything to do with the missing tops?" I ask Bhima suddenly.

"*Moi?*" Bhima says from the bed.

Feeling utterly relieved that I won't ever have to see Ted again, I take a shower, brush my teeth, and slip under the duvet with Charlie and Bhima.

"At least I know I can feel at least a little attraction to another human being," I say, turning toward the side of the bed Bhima slept in, feeling calm once again.

"True," Bhima says. "And Ted's a lucky guy."

"How so?"

"He got to hold your hand."

CHAPTER 53

"Hallo, darling!
"Hallo, Mum."

"David Starling called and said, 'They're giving COVIS vaccines in Tangmere,' so we jumped in the car and went and got it!"

"That's wonderful!" I say. Then, "Have you had any side effects?"

"None at all," Mum says. She sounds delighted.

"What a relief!" I say. "Now I won't have to worry about you so much!"

Mum giggles. She sounds like a teenager. "Oh, darling, were you worried? That's nice."

Sure I'm worried. They're eighty-eight and eighty-nine years old, Dad is almost completely deaf now, Mum's memory isn't what it used to be, they haven't seen their friends in months, and they keep forgetting to wear their masks.

Sure I'm worried.

"Shall I come and see you?"

"Oh, you mustn't come, darling. Because of COVIS. Much too risky. Don't worry. We'll be fine."

The phone rings again. It's Bob. "You're getting vaccinated next week, Alison."

"Why?" I say.

"Because you're my aide."

"I'm not your aide!"

"You drive me around a lot. So you're my aide. So the people in my building say you gotta have a vaccine . . ."

Bob lives in subsidized housing for people over sixty-five, or as he calls it, The Home for the Nearly Departed, which is across the road from my house.

I go to a school gym in Pittsfield, stand in line with hundreds of other people in masks, wait at a little desk for ten minutes, get the vaccine and the vaccine card which is signed and dated and feel a deep sense of relief.

It appears I am going to live.

To celebrate, I head to Berkshire Bike and Board and buy an electric bike. I call it the Yellow Bird and I ride it down to the coffee shop, along Route 7 to the supermarket, up Monument Valley Road toward Beartown State Park, down into Great Barrington, and back and forth between Stockbridge and Lenox.

One morning, I arrive at the coffee shop, and, to my surprise, not only are all the Bobs there, but Alan is too. Usually they come at different times, but not on this occasion.

"Hi, guys," I say. "What's up?"

"You were going down the hill from Lenox to Stockbridge and you broke the speed limit. You're ridin' way too fast."

"It's not safe, Alison. You need to slow down. We all chipped in and we got you this," one of the Bobs says, handing me a yellow reflector jacket and a pair of gloves.

"Thanks guys," I say.

"And here's a helmet. It's my spare," Alan says. "I wore it when I biked across the country."

"You want me to wear a helmet?" I say in disbelief.

They're all looking at me.

"Okay. Okay. Okay. I'll wear it. Thanks guys."

❋ ❋ ❋

As soon as I get my booster shot, I am on a plane to England to see my parents for the first time since they met Bhima.

A week before the pandemic started, Mum and Dad bought a tiny one-bedroom flat with the intention of fixing it up, renting it out to actors from the Chichester Festival Theatre, then moving somewhere with a garden and a bedroom for visitors soon thereafter.

They moved in the day before lockdown.

Then, like everyone else, they were locked down. For two years.

In a tiny flat. With nothing else for company but a television blaring terrifying news at them day after day after day.

They seem thinner. And much older.

Dad's hearing is even worse than it was last time I saw them. And Mum, who used to love to cook, now feeds the two of them frozen meals from Marks & Spencer, which she heats up in the toaster oven for lunch and supper.

The fridge is not clean. Neither is the bathroom.

They are both in the early stages of dementia.

"We're fine," Mum says.

They're not.

The flat is so small there isn't room for me to stay there, so I stay at the Travelodge, which is about a five-minute walk away.

I join them for toast and marmalade in the mornings, then walk around Chichester, sometimes alone, sometimes very slowly, with Dad.

Dad is so deaf now, there's not much talking to be done between us, and he's unsteady on his feet.

At the end of the day I stand up, ready to return to the Travelodge. Dad stands up too.

"I'll walk you over there," Dad says.

"It's alright, Dad, I'm fine. This is Chichester, not the Bronx."

"No. I'm coming. To protect you from the nasty men."

"What nasty men?"

Dad has been watching the news which is full of stories about women being attacked on the streets by nasty men.

"They're not here in Chichester, Dad!" I shout. "Besides I'd like to see them try. I've lived in America for almost thirty years. I'd punch them in the nose. Or shoot 'em."

"Nonsense," Dad says, insisting.

Dad shuffles slow and unsteady along the street. I walk next to him. What would have taken me four minutes to walk takes us half an hour. When we finally get to the door of the Travelodge, Dad says, "I'll stay here until I know you're safely inside."

I walk towards the entrance and wave at him.

I peer out the window. As soon as I see him turn his back, I cross the road behind him and follow him back until he's safely home with the woman he's been so happily married to for sixty-five years.

"Have you thought about getting a walking stick, Dad?" I say casually the next day.

"WHAT?"

I buy him a maroon walking stick from the mobility shop in Little London. Maybe if I wrap it up and give it to him as a birthday present he'll accept it.

He loves it. He has a merry time pulling it up and down. It helps steady him.

"Perhaps you'd like a cleaner too? Or someone to help with shopping?"

"Nonsense!" Mum says, as furious with me for suggesting they might need a cleaner as she is with my brothers for telling them it's time to stop driving the car.

"What an idiotic suggestion!" Dad says, suddenly joining in. "Really!"

I have a quick memory of my often impatient, very clever father trying to teach me multiplication.

"No, Alison! Six times six is thirty-six, not forty-six, you idiot!"

I used to get upset when Dad called me an idiot because I couldn't do the things that he could do well. Like tidying up and being good at math. But not anymore.

We don't have much time.

All that matters is loving him as he is now.

As I'm leaving to go back to America, Dad takes me by the elbow and into his little office next to the sitting room.

"We've only got enough money for Mum to go into a home," he says quietly. "Not enough for both of us. My mind's going. I'm finished. Have you got any cyanide?" he asks, hopefully.

"Sorry, Dad, no. I don't have any on me at the moment."

"Never mind," Dad says as he pats me on the shoulder.

"Do you love us?" Dad says later as I am heading out the door.

"Very much!" I say.

"We love you too!" Dad says. "Very much!"

I hug him goodbye, aware that I've never heard him use the "L" word before.

We are, after all, English.

CHAPTER 54

When I get home, Bhima, who gave all his spare money to the Second Chance Animal Shelter, informs me that he's set me up on a date with a veterinarian called Frank.

"Are you coming with me?" I ask.

"I am," Bhima says, reaching for his coat as we head out the door and into the car.

Frank is tall and thin with white hair. He's wearing a long-sleeve shirt and jeans. He's sitting on the wall outside the restaurant watching me as I park, unaware of the Indian gentleman right by my side.

I know Frank is hopeful. Everyone who goes on an online date is hopeful. "Is this the person I'm looking for? Is THIS the person? Is THIS the one?"

"I dunno, Bhima," I say, as we approach Frank.

"Stay open," Bhima says.

I smile and shake Frank's floppy hand and sit at a table. I let him buy me a cup of herbal tea. Pronounced without the "H." The American way.

Frank seems nice enough, and while it is true that he doesn't have all his teeth, he does have most of them.

He begins by telling me, at great length, why he's retiring early.

"Funny thing is," Frank says, "even though I've been a vet for forty years, I've never really liked animals all that much."

"That is *funny*!" I say, laughing.

He looks at me askance.

Oh, dear. He's not joking.

He continues by telling me earnestly why you should never—ever—ever adopt a dog that's older than nine weeks.

"They got problems," he says. "The adopted dogs, like adopted kids, they got nothing but problems. You get what you pay for. What you want is a puppy. I've got access to the best. They're a good deal, three thousand each. Labs—reliably pure-bred—if you're interested."

Bhima is sitting at a table opposite with his head in his hands.

I want nothing more than to find out this is all part of a bad dream, and all I have to do is hold Bhima's hand and walk with him out, out, out into the clean air.

"Oh, dear," I say, looking at my phone suddenly.

"Everything okay?" Frank says.

"It's my friend Sasha. She's in trouble. Yikes!"

He stands, concerned.

"Want me to come with you?"

"No. NO!" I say. "No. No, no, no. She's—I—sorry. Thank you so much for the tea. But I've really got to go."

I run across the parking lot to my car.

Without a word, Bhima hands me my phone.

Dear Frank,

I'm so sorry, you're a very nice chap. But I don't think we are a match.

I wish you nothing but the best.

Alison

* * *

I agree to meet Sam Porter at the Haven Café in Lenox because he assures me, over text, that he dislikes watching American football and basketball as much as I do.

He's tall and attractive, with a mop of black curly hair and very pale skin.

"So you're into Chinese medicine?" I say.

"It saved my life, actually."

"How so?"

I am greatly enjoying the Haven special. And the fact that Sam was willing to meet me first thing in the morning so we could have breakfast, which is my time of day.

"When I was in my forties I had this heart condition," he says.

Oh, no.

"I found this doctor in Vermont. He asked me questions and gave me really smelly teas. At first I was skeptical, but they worked. My cholesterol came way down, my doctors couldn't believe the numbers. Now I'm great! No one's heard of this guy, he lives on a hill in the middle of nowhere, but . . ."

"You mean Dr. Li?" I interrupt.

"You know him?"

"Yes," I say.

I've already told Sam that I was very much in love with a man who died suddenly. But I didn't tell him where Bhima lived.

"Dr. Li lived five minutes from Bhima's house," I say. "I tried to get Bhima to see him. But Bhima thought Eastern medicine was a crock, so he wouldn't go."

"Whaaaaaaat?" Sam says, his eyes alight with something akin to wonder. "I tried to get my wife to go there, but she refused. Then she died!"

"In the adoption world, what some people call coincidence, we call it synchronicity. It happens all the time," I say, chomping into my French toast. "As my Tennessean grandfather said to me just before he died, 'There ain't no such thing as coincidence.'"

Then Sam tells me he's into astrology. And I'm back with Bhima, on his last night on earth, looking up through the telescope at the stars.

I close my eyes for a second. The sky is dark. The stars are bright. There's an eerie light in the woods nearby. As if the woods know it is time to say goodbye to the gentle, strong Indian who kept the hunters away during his time living in that small patch of Vermont.

If we are made from stardust,
A star is what we are,
Perhaps you have gone back up there?
If you have it's awfully far.

Come to think of it, where is Bhima right now?

I look around. No sign of Bhima at the Haven Café. That's

unusual.

I return my full attention to Sam.

When we stand up to leave, Sam bends down and picks up a penny. "This means she's speaking to me," he says.

"Who?"

"My wife. The penny on the ground. That's how they send a sign."

He probably believes in white feathers, too.

Hey, whatever it takes.

"Come and see my house next time?" Sam says.

"Sure."

There's some kind of connection.

Could Sam be the soulmate the Arch was praying for?

When I get home Bhima's not there either. But Charlie is, and he squeals and jumps about until I pick him up in my arms and tell him he is my favorite dog in the whole world.

CHAPTER 55

Sam lives in Shelburne Falls, in a maroon and gray Queen Anne-style house with peaky roofs and turrets. There are overgrown flowers outside the house, and beds for a vegetable garden that looks like it hasn't been tended in years.

Sam is sitting in a rocking chair on the front porch in a checked shirt and blue jeans watching Charlie and me arrive. He looks languid.

Charlie and I head into his house. It's dark, the windows are small, and there's a smell I can't identify that's, well, a tad rancid actually, combined with incense maybe.

"Stay open," I tell myself.

The furniture is wooden, covered in dark pink velvet, and there's a wood-burning stove in the center of the living room.

There are also astrology cards on the walls. Giant ones. I mean, maybe five-by-three feet.

"Hey, I did your chart by the way," Sam says.

"Did you discover anything interesting?"

"You have moon in Cancer and your rising sign is Gemini," he says, looking at me significantly. "We're a perfect fit."

"Ah," I say.

I have absolutely no idea what this means, and to be honest, I don't believe people's life paths are predetermined by the stars—or by anything, for that matter.

As Sam tells me more about how right we are for each other, I am aware that Bhima has just shown up.

I can see him walking toward me on the other side of the window, through the sunlight, walking over a field and past a broken fire pit. I'm relieved to see him. I haven't seen him in days.

The light outside the window contrasts with the darkness inside the house.

We're sitting at Sam's long wooden kitchen table eating lentil soup when Charlie jumps and runs barking into a small room we haven't entered yet. I follow him into a room where boxes and books take up most of the floor space. Then I hear a rustling sound.

"What's that?" I say.

Charlie has figured it out and is standing, hackles raised, staring at several large rats in a cage.

"Hey!" Sam says. "Those are my pet rats. Want me to take them out so you can pet them?"

"Not unless you'd like Charlie to eat them," I say.

Charlie is growling at the rats as Bhima says, "Ask him some more questions about his wife."

So I do.

"My wife didn't believe in monogamy," Sam says, "so she had love affairs with the neighbors."

"Were you alright with that?"

"It was the only way I could keep her, so yeah. Sometimes her lovers came over for dinner with the kids."

"How did your kids handle that?"

"Very well. She was real close to all three of them. And she was really there for my daughters when they started cutting themselves."

"Why did they do that?"

"Because they didn't want to have sex, like the other girls at school."

"Nothing to do with their mom sleeping with the neighbors then?"

He looks at me as if I'm parochial somehow.

"Of course not."

Then he tells me that the only woman he has been with since his wife died five years ago was a Wiccan who cast a spell on him. Then he asks me if I want to get high.

Bhima's ready to leave and so am I. When I open the door, Charlie dashes out and heads for the car at top speed.

"Hey! Yo! Charlie!" Sam calls from the door. He sounds

annoyed.

"What is it?" I say.

"Your dog pissed in my shoe!"

"I'm sorry. So sorry. Sorry! I'll chastise him immediately! Charlie!" I say, getting into the car and waving at Sam who is holding a wet sneaker in his limp hand as we drive away.

As soon as I am sure we are out of earshot I say, "Well DONE, Charlie! Well DONE!"

This time Bhima does the typing.

Dear Sam,

You're a lovely chap. But I don't think we are a match.

I wish you nothing but the best,

Alison

CHAPTER 56

It's late spring 2022. I'm out as much as I can be, walking. Biking. Breathing in the Berkshire air. And writing *Grief . . . A Comedy*.

As I bike through the Berkshire Hills, seeing the world from the seat of my bicycle changes everything. I realize I have fallen in love. With the trees and the daffodils and the air and the mountains and the people around me.

The extra energy I felt soon after Bhima died fills me again with something akin to joy.

The only thing that comes near it, in my experience, is what happens after the pain of childbirth. It's the most excruciating thing in the world and yet following that terrible pain you get this deep sense of love, connection, and joy.

Without the pain you wouldn't have the kids.

"I wish I knew where you were when you're not with me," I say to Bhima as I'm looking at the stars one night. "If I knew you were alright . . ."

That night, I have the most vivid dream.

I am sitting on the floor with Bhima's family in his house in Vermont. Bhima's mother is wearing a sari, his sister too, his brothers are also dressed in traditional Indian clothing. I am wearing the turquoise silk top and loose white Indian pants that Bhima bought me. The sun is setting outside and there is sadness in the air.

I'm sitting cross-legged with my back against the sofa, facing the kitchen window, behind which are the blueberry bushes Bhima and I ate from every day they were in fruit at the end of our last summer.

Suddenly the wall on that side of Bhima's house disappears,

revealing a brightly colored world bathed in bright gold and orange light. I can hear music—light and pure.

I can see Bhima walking toward us down a golden-yellow path that's surrounded by pink and red flowers. He looks radiant in silk Indian clothing and he's with a beautiful young Indian woman who's dressed in orange, turquoise, and gold. They are so happy to be with each other and there is such joy and peace and love coming from and between both of them.

At first I think, "Hey, Bhima, that didn't take you long." Then I realize it isn't a romantic relationship. I somehow know that the woman has been waiting for him for some time, that he had to complete some sort of task before he could come to her, and they are both ecstatic.

She has extra hands and is somehow connected to a tiger resting near bright pink flowers in green grass under the shade of a small tree with a white trunk.

The woman has an intense glow about her and now I can see that Bhima is there because she needs him to help her with something. He seems to be in a position of seniority, but she is in charge.

Everything in this world is filled with love and light. Everything.

They don't look at me directly, but as I look at them I am touched by light and a love so powerful it fills every part of my being.

Still absorbed in each other, I watch them go over to the fireplace in Bhima's house. There's a fire burning and they turn slightly away from us, looking into the flames, aware of us but not looking directly at Bhima's family or me. We are all sitting in Bhima's living room that is now filled with this powerful radiant light, near them but coming from a different world.

I know in that moment that Bhima has moved far, far, far beyond the human frame that limited him so much when he was on earth. That he left because he was urgently needed in the world right next to this one, to help with things I cannot begin to understand.

When I told Bhima's sister about the dream she asked me what the woman looked like. I told her and Bhima's sister emailed me a photograph and said, "Was this the woman?"

The photo she sent was of a woman identical to the one in the dream.

"He's with Durga," Bhima's sister said when I told her, sounding quite matter-of-fact.

Who?

"She's a Hindu goddess. She symbolizes feminine positive energy and strength. She is known as the great protector. My father was a devotee. Bhima used to go with him to temple when he was a boy, but didn't take any of it seriously. Maybe something rubbed off."

When Bhima's mother heard about my dream, she said, "Why did Durga come to Alison and not one of us? I'll tell you why. Because Alison doesn't know a bloody thing about Durga or Hinduism, so we know it's real since she can't possibly have imagined it. We can be at peace. We know Bhima is with Durga now. Alison is blessed."

When I talk to Bhima's younger brother, who knows a lot more about Hinduism than me (which isn't hard since I truly know nothing), I tell him I don't understand why Bhima and Durga headed for the fireplace and waited there, turned partially away, looking at the glowing fire.

"In Hindu religion the gods and goddesses communicate with the living through fire," he tells me.

A few weeks later I go into Asia Barong, a local antique store where I find a framed picture of Durga. She's in a world very similar to the one I saw in my dream, only this time she's riding on the back of a tiger.

I hang the painting at the bottom of my stairs at home and imagine Bhima there. Surrounded by light. Radiant. Ecstatically happy.

I glance over at the little maroon velvet bag with a few of Bhima's ashes in it that's been sitting on my writing desk for the past two years.

"Why am I so happy?" I ask myself aloud.

My daughter is home from college for the weekend, and she's overheard me.

"I know," Lucy says, flipping on the kettle that used to live in Bhima's kitchen and now lives in mine.

"Okay, clever clogs, tell me?" I say.

"I've been doing this course on the neuroscience of love," she says. "I think all the love you had for Bhima stayed inside you when he died," Lucy says. "So even though Bhima left you, physically, the love didn't. I mean, love is energy, right?"

"You sound just like him," I say.

How Bhima would have loved the people my children have become.

"I think loving Bhima changed your neurological pathways for good," Lucy says. "So now that you know love is nothing to be afraid of, you can be wide open to it in a whole new way. I mean, love comes in all shapes and forms, right?"

"Yes, my little wise one."

Now that I know how quickly life can end, I don't want to miss a minute, so I've learned how to really listen—to the people at the coffee shop, to my friends, to my son, and perhaps especially to my daughter, to whom I am giving my full attention these days.

"Love is the only thing that matters," I say, quoting Nick again. "That, and connection. Because it's only in connection that love can find expression."

"That's right, Mom," Lucy says. "You need to do more of the connecting thing. You've been spending waaaay too much time alone."

She takes her tea over to the couch, opens her laptop and is soon engrossed in writing her essay.

I take my tea over to the couch, open my laptop and am soon engrossed in the final script edits of *Grief . . . A Comedy*, the one-woman show. Rehearsals start in just over a week.

❋ ❋ ❋

Two days later, on May 5, 2022, I'm woken by the ringing of the phone at 6:00 a.m. It's my brother Peter letting me know that Dad just died.

In the moment I hear of his passing, I picture my Dad quite clearly. He's no longer trapped in his tired, aging body, deaf and scarcely able to move. Instead, he's a young boy again, running fast and free through an English field, vaulting a gate, laughing with joy. He's wearing gray shorts and a white shirt.

I email Jim Frangione and the others at the theater, tell them my Dad's died and I'm very sorry but I must cancel the show.

Then I rummage about in the filing cabinet for my passport, sling some clothes over my left arm, grab my toothbrush, chuck the lot in the back of the car and head for the airport.

"I wish you could be with me, I mean really," I say to Bhima as I drive, thinking of my father and my family in England who need me now.

CHAPTER 57

When I arrive at her flat, Mum looks frail and a little bit lost. My brothers have been with her, but now that I'm here they're going home to their wives.

I know how hard the first few days can be. Poor Mum.

"Thank you for coming, darling," Mum says as I hug her.

Over the next three days, I sleep on the sofa bed and do a little shopping and cooking and never leave her side.

She looks a little confused from time to time. But she doesn't cry.

On the fourth day I sit on the sofa that Dad loved to lie on, doing the crossword, dozing and reading the paper.

I show Mum the poster for *Grief...A Comedy*, and then she asks me to read her the script.

Mum is utterly present, listening carefully as I take her through the love story of Bhima and me, ending with the final song that I wrote only last week, after a bike ride in the Berkshire Hills.

As I get to the second half, I am aware that Mum is clutching my hand.

"Darling! I'm so sorry," she says when I get to the end, her eyes full of tears. "If it hadn't been for this silly COVIS we'd have come to the funeral. We'd have come to be with you when . . ."

"I know."

"Thank you, darling."

"What for?"

"Dad and I had sixty-five very, very happy years together. But you and Bhima . . . oh, darling, you were only just getting started. I'm so sorry. How lucky Dad and I were—how very very

lucky. And I—I quite agree. We mustn't waste a minute of whatever time we have left. When do you start performing *Grief . . .
A Comedy?*"

"Rehearsals were supposed to start on Monday, but I've
canceled the show, Mum."

"Why?"

"So I could be here to look after you!"

"That's ridiculous!" she says.

"I've made the decision, Mum," I say.

I'm tired, so I hug her goodnight, and fall into a deep sleep.

In the morning I wake up and open my laptop to a slew of
emails.

"Great news, Alison. See you Monday!" says Jim Frangione.

"FANTASTIC!" from the publicist.

"Thank God!" from Tristan, the theater's managing director,
who already had a sold-out house.

Huh?

A message from my director clarifies things. "I had a lovely
talk with your Mum," he says. "She's hilarious. After telling us
you'll be back in time to start rehearsals, she said she's planning
on helping you write a sequel. *Grief . . . A Comedy, Part Two,* all
about your Dad."

My Mum said . . . what???

I look up and there's Mum standing in the doorway wearing
her white Marks & Spencer nightie and Dad's slippers.

"Dad would be furious with both of us if you canceled the
show now," she says. "So I called the theater and told them you'd
be doing it after all."

"Oh, Mum. Are you sure? Are you really alright?"

"I will be," she says. Then, "Now, hurry darling! The taxi will
be here any minute now."

Mum hands me my hairbrush and says, "I found it under
the dressing table. Don't forget to brush your hair!"

CHAPTER 58

We have a two-week rehearsal period with the director James Warwick, the costume designer, and the stage manager all wearing masks.

I'm not alone on stage because Gary is sitting at the piano at the back every single night.

I perform the show, becoming Bhima on stage, then me, then Bhima again, sharing our story with the people sitting in front of me.

Some of them are strangers. Some of them are friends, family, and colleagues who have flown from as far away as LA, London, and even Hong Kong to see the show.

The Bobs all come. So do Jessica and Amy from the coffee shop. So does my hiking buddy Sarah and Alex the massage therapist and Mark and Pops from the hair salon.

So do little Eden's mother and Marina's family. So do Maria and Nicole and Vicki and Bhima's friends and family members.

And each night when I sing the final song, I know that I'm not just singing about me. I'm singing about all of us.

> I can walk. I can breathe! I can speak
> And see and hear, and I can bend my knees.
> I've got two legs, I find things funny, and if
> I keep my living simple, I've got enough money.
> I can read any book, I can eat Feta cheese,
> There are people I love who are living, I can spend
> time with these.
> It's not the life I thought I'd live, but I'm good at
> changing plans, I've got

A lot to be thankful for
And a likely long life span.
And when I'm missing my true love
If I get very still
And close my eyes and take a breath I can
Bring him near at will
I can walk, I can breathe
I can shut out all distractions
And take the time to grieve
And if grieving is the price we pay
For the deep love that we feel
Then grief is just part of the deal
Yes grief is just part of the deal.

CHAPTER 59

A month later I am on a plane to Montana with Bhima's ashes in my pocket, in the little maroon velvet bag that Bhima's family gave me with a little bit of Bhima in it.

My plan is to scatter Bhima's ashes at the highest peak on the last day of our five-day hike in Glacier National Park.

There are maybe twenty other people on the hike, from all over the world. We're with Climate Ride, raising money for organizations that help combat climate change. I'm hiking for Green Vermont, which was one of Bhima's favorite charities.

We hike fifteen to twenty miles each day. We pitch our little tents in the midst of the Rocky Mountains. With my head resting on the sweatshirt I'm using for a pillow, I unzip the ceiling flaps of my tent so I can fall asleep looking at the stars.

At about 8:00 a.m. on the final day, I'm standing under a tent putting my sandwich into a brown paper bag. Suddenly, there's a strong gust of wind that blows the paper bag I'm holding out of my hand.

I run after the flyaway sandwich bag just as the wind lifts the heavy tent high up into the air. And as I reach for that bag, the steel tent poles come crashing down to where my head would have been.

The other hikers and staff are crowding around, astonished. "Alison!" they say, "That wind just saved your life!"

I curl my hand around the little velvet pouch with Bhima's ashes in it that's resting in my pocket and look up at the awesome mountains.

That's when I glimpse Bhima and Durga for a moment, full of joy, twirling victoriously in the wind.

"Thank you," I whisper. And then they're gone.

I breathe in the mountain air. Then I breathe out again.

And I know, in that moment, that I will not waste one minute of whatever time I've got left.

The sun kisses my face as I tighten the hiking boots Bhima gave me in preparation for the climb ahead.

And when I return home, a dachshund runs into my arms, as an Indian gentleman watches from the shadows.

❋ ❋ ❋

There will be people, like me, some days, who think I've imagined all this.

There will be others, like me, some days, who think my visits from Bhima literally happen.

I believe different things at different times.

But I'm absolutely sure of one thing. And it's this:

When someone we deeply love dies, a part of who they were becomes a part of who we are now.

So if I'm right, and there's a part of Bhima that's inside the me that is writing the final sentences of this book right now, let me leave you with a few words from him.

"The answer, Alison, is renewable energy. And for God's sake, I don't care if it's the end of a long day! You must recycle everything!"

So I did.

POSTSCRIPT

Dec 6, 2023

Dear Arch,

The night of the first performance of *Grief . . . A Comedy* in London, I was waiting backstage at the Soho Theatre in my pink shirt and jeans, i.e. my costume, peeking through a hole in the curtain at the audience. The room was packed with strangers mostly, but I could see my family and old friends from different stages of the English life that I've missed so much.

And was that you wearing a jaunty black cap, sitting with Dad and Bhima on the bench to the right of the stage?

Either way, you were right. People who had lost loved ones came to London to see the show from all over the country. I got to meet some of them in the bar afterwards and plucked up the courage to ask if they too had felt their loved ones near them after they died.

A librarian from Winchester looked at me with an expression of relief, burst into tears, nodded vigorously and said, "Thank you for asking the question."

A retired math teacher from Leeds told me that she lays a place for her deceased husband every night at dinner, and has done since he died three years ago. "We talk, just like we always did."

And then we were all talking at once, finishing each other's sentences.

It could be true.

It could be wishful thinking.

It could be something in between.

But if death isn't an ending at all, but really just a shift in energy . . . if we are spiritual beings having a human experience . . . if the people we love who have died really are filled with light and love and peace in a radiant, color-filled world right next to this one . . . well, doesn't that change everything?

So, I've written a show and now this book and I've kept my promise to you to do what I can to tell this story as widely as possible.

Now it seems I'm out of isolation and Bhima and I are off on a world tour. Did you have anything to do with that?

By the way, I was wondering, is there any progress on finding me a new soulmate?

If possible, once I've completed my task, I'd so appreciate it if you could help me find me someone I can truly love who is alive and likely to remain so.

It would also be great if they could be cheerful, a good rummy player, and strong enough to help me carry my luggage.

Ubuntu.

Alison

ACKNOWLEDGMENTS

Thank you to Archbishop Desmond Tutu, for encouraging me to tell this story. Thank you to Trevor Dolby, my literary agent and co-conspirator, for sharing my fondness for breaking the rules and leading the way. Thank you to my UK manager Richard Bucknall, Mark Godfrey, David Luff and the team at the Soho Theatre, for stepping up and bringing *Grief . . . A Comedy* (the show), for real, to London, Edinburgh, and beyond. Thank you to Gary Schreiner for writing the music and coming with me on this journey. Thank you to my writer friends who encouraged me to finish this book, especially Tony Eprile, Judith Schwartz, Peter Buckman, Natalie Boyce, Erik Bruun, and Jana Laiz.

Thank you to my early editors Beth Heidi Adelman and Eliza Keenan.

Thank you to my friends at Stockbridge Coffee and Tea, including Bob, Bob, Bob, Alan, Roger, Nick, Paul, John, Jessica, Amy, Noah, Kasha, Jonah, and Abbey.

Thank you to my beautiful children and Bhima's family and friends for their love and kindness.

Thank you to my "rescue" dachshund Charlie. Who rescued who?

Thank you, especially, to Sita, for her love, encouragement, and blessings.

And thank you to my beloved Bhima. For everything.